THIS NEW OLD BOOK IS DEDICATED TO:

Laura Varsky – God bless you!,

Alberto Breccia and Oski.

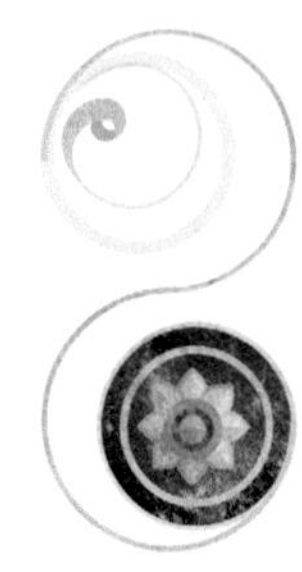

I'D LIKE TO THANK DIE GESTALTEN'S PEOPLE FOR THIS OPPORTUNITY.

GOD BLESS YOU!

THE CREATION

Pictures from the Book of Genesis

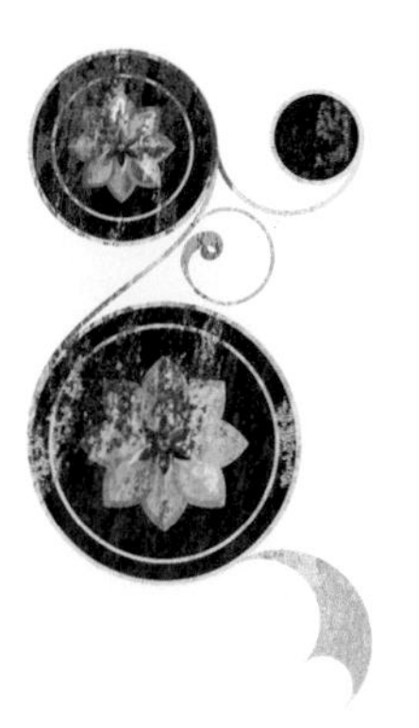

by Christian Montenegro

THE BEGINNING

[1] In the beginning God created the heavens and the earth. [2] Now the earth was formless and empty, darkness was over the surface of the deep, and the Spirit of God was hovering over the waters.
[3] And God said, "Let there be light," and there was light. [4] God saw that the light was good, and he separated the light from the darkness. [5] God called the light "day," and the darkness he called "night." And there was evening, and there was morning – the first day.

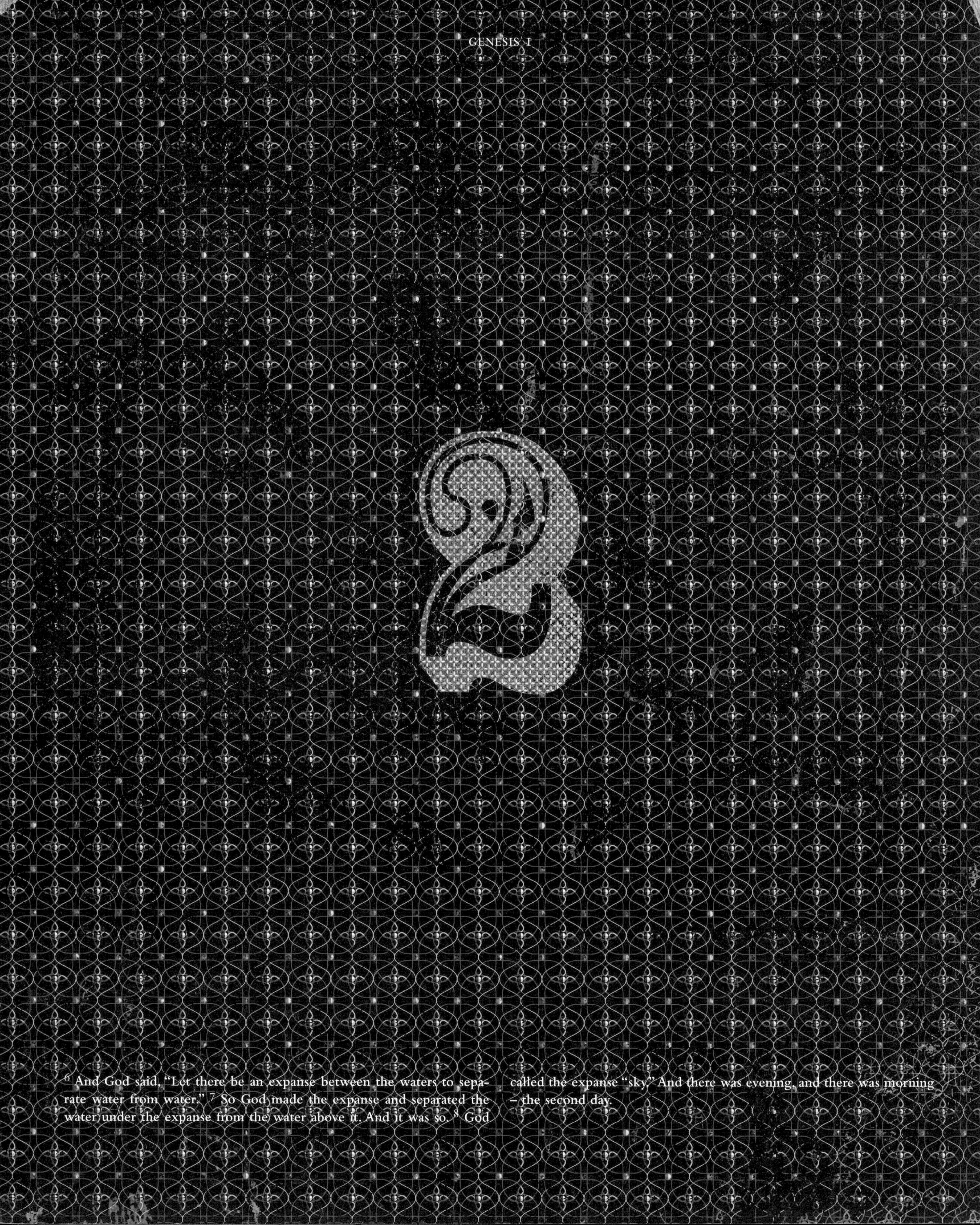

[6] And God said, "Let there be an expanse between the waters to separate water from water." [7] So God made the expanse and separated the water under the expanse from the water above it. And it was so. [8] God called the expanse "sky." And there was evening, and there was morning – the second day.

[9] And God said, "Let the water under the sky be gathered to one place, and let dry ground appear." And it was so. [10] God called the dry ground "land," and the gathered waters he called "seas." And God saw that it was good.

[11] Then God said, "Let the land produce vegetation: seed-bearing plants and trees on the land that bear fruit with seed in it, according to their various kinds." And it was so. [12] The land produced vegetation: plants bearing seed according to their kinds and trees bearing fruit with seed in it according to their kinds. And God saw that it was good. [13] And there was evening, and there was morning – the third day.

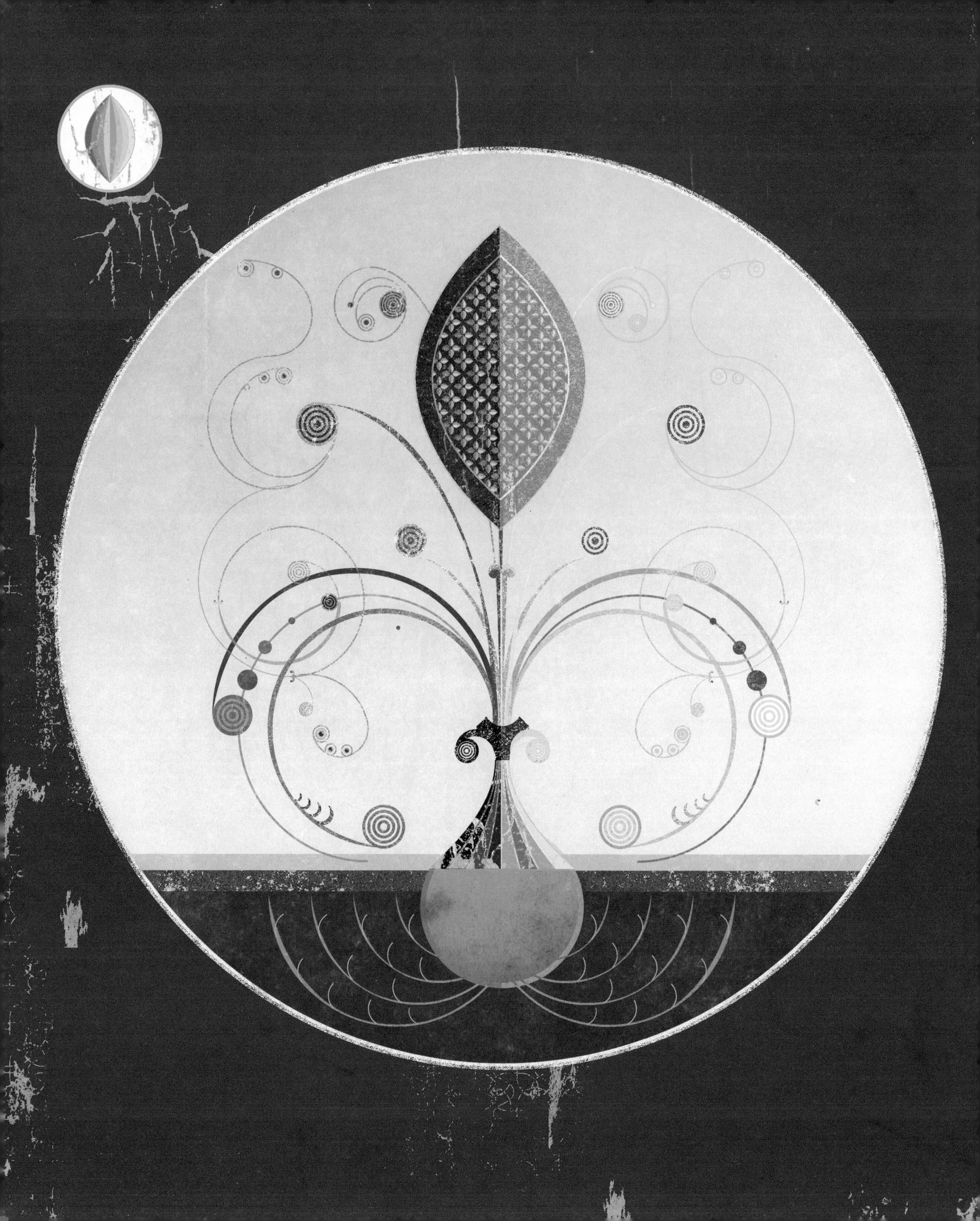

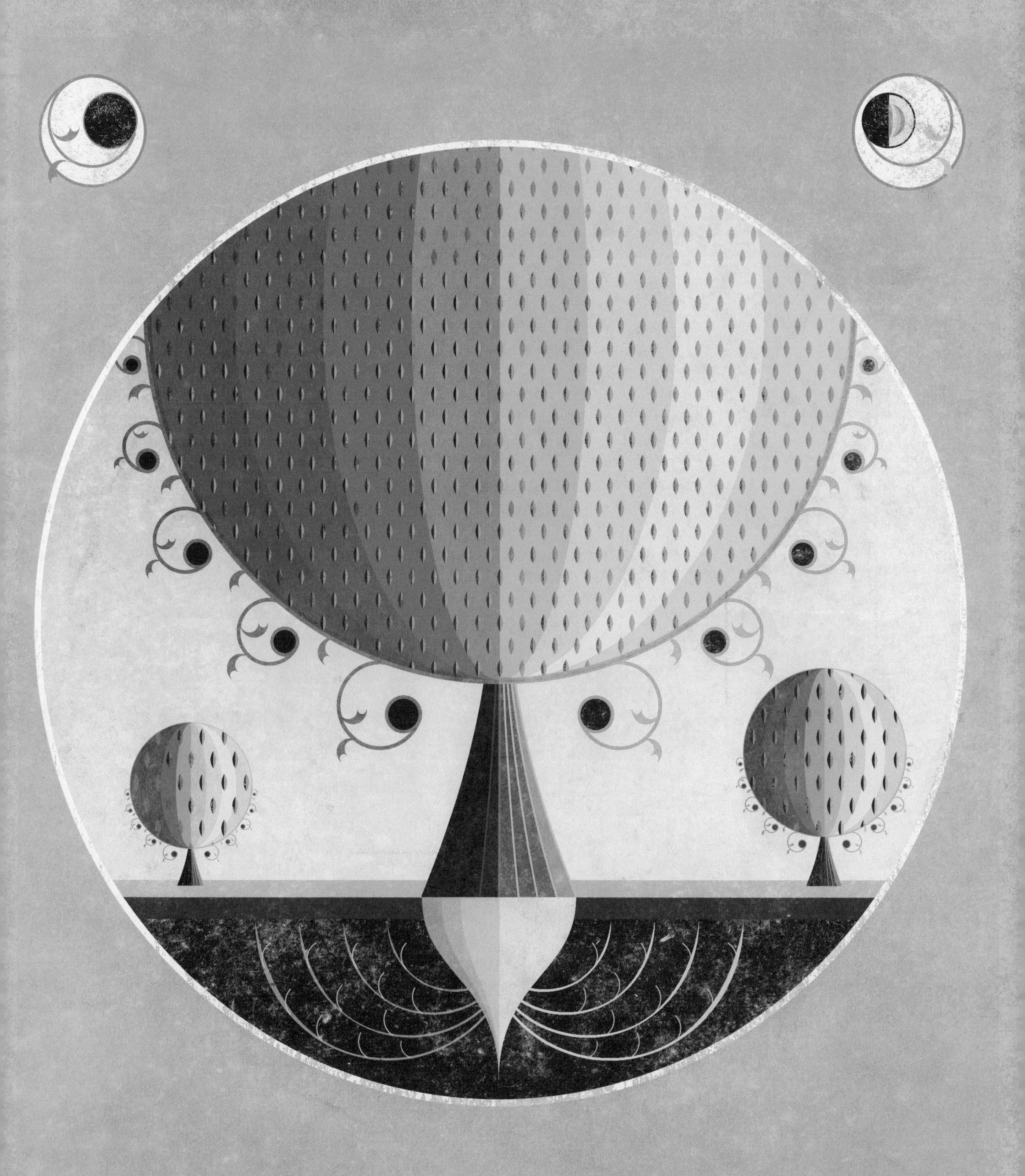

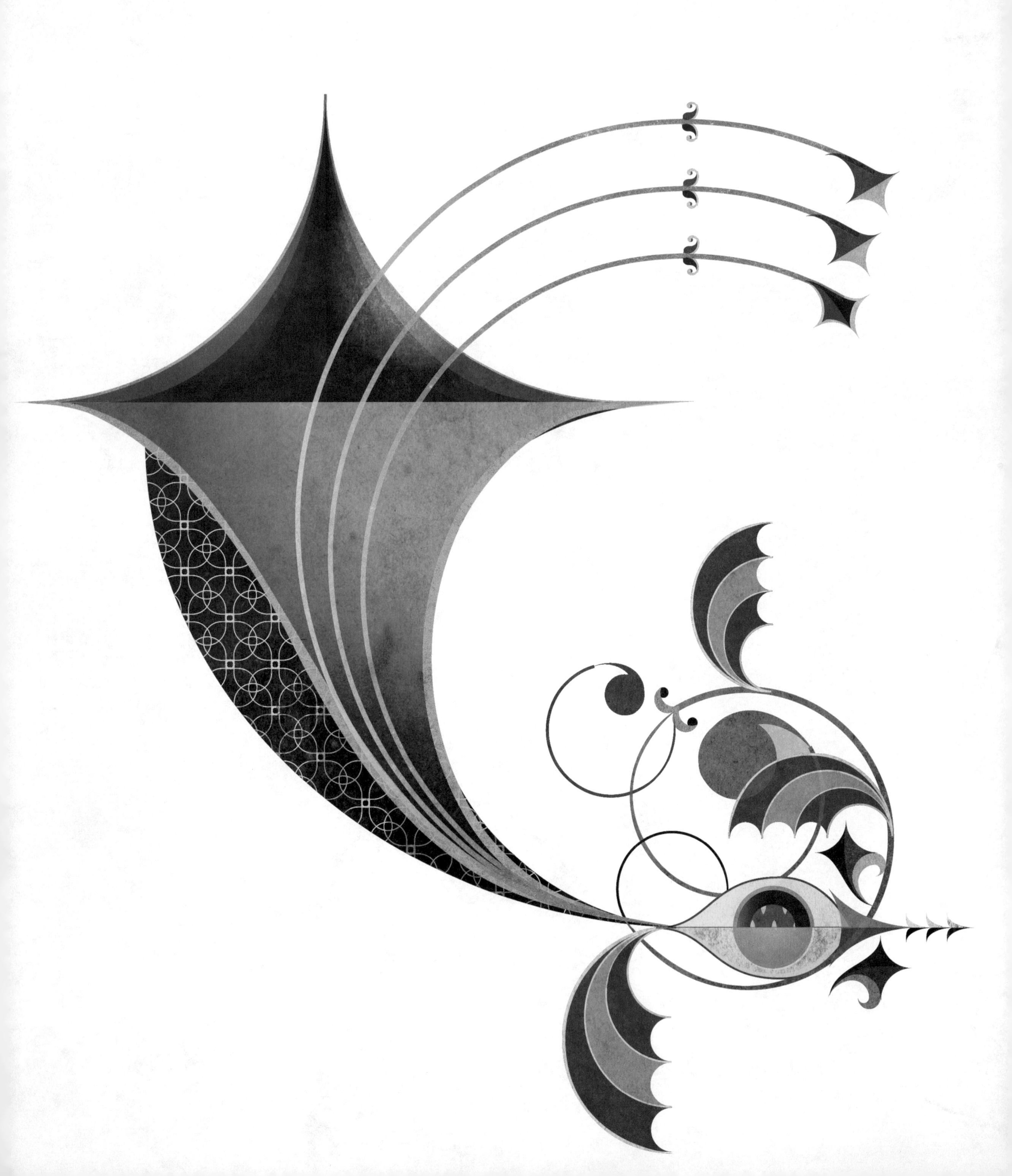

[14] And God said, "Let there be lights in the expanse of the sky to separate the day from the night, and let them serve as signs to mark seasons and days and years, [15] and let them be lights in the expanse of the sky to give light on the earth." And it was so. [16] God made two great lights – the greater light to govern the day and the lesser light to govern the night. He also made the stars. [17] God set them in the expanse of the sky to give light on the earth, [18] to govern the day and the night, and to separate light from darkness. And God saw that it was good. [19] And there was evening, and there was morning – the fourth day.

[20] And God said, "Let the water teem with living creatures, and let birds fly above the earth across the expanse of the sky." [21] So God created the great creatures of the sea and every living and moving thing with which the water teems, according to their kinds, and every winged bird according to its kind. And God saw that it was good. [22] God blessed them and said, "Be fruitful and increase in number and fill the water in the seas, and let the birds increase on the earth." [23] And there was evening, and there was morning – the fifth day.

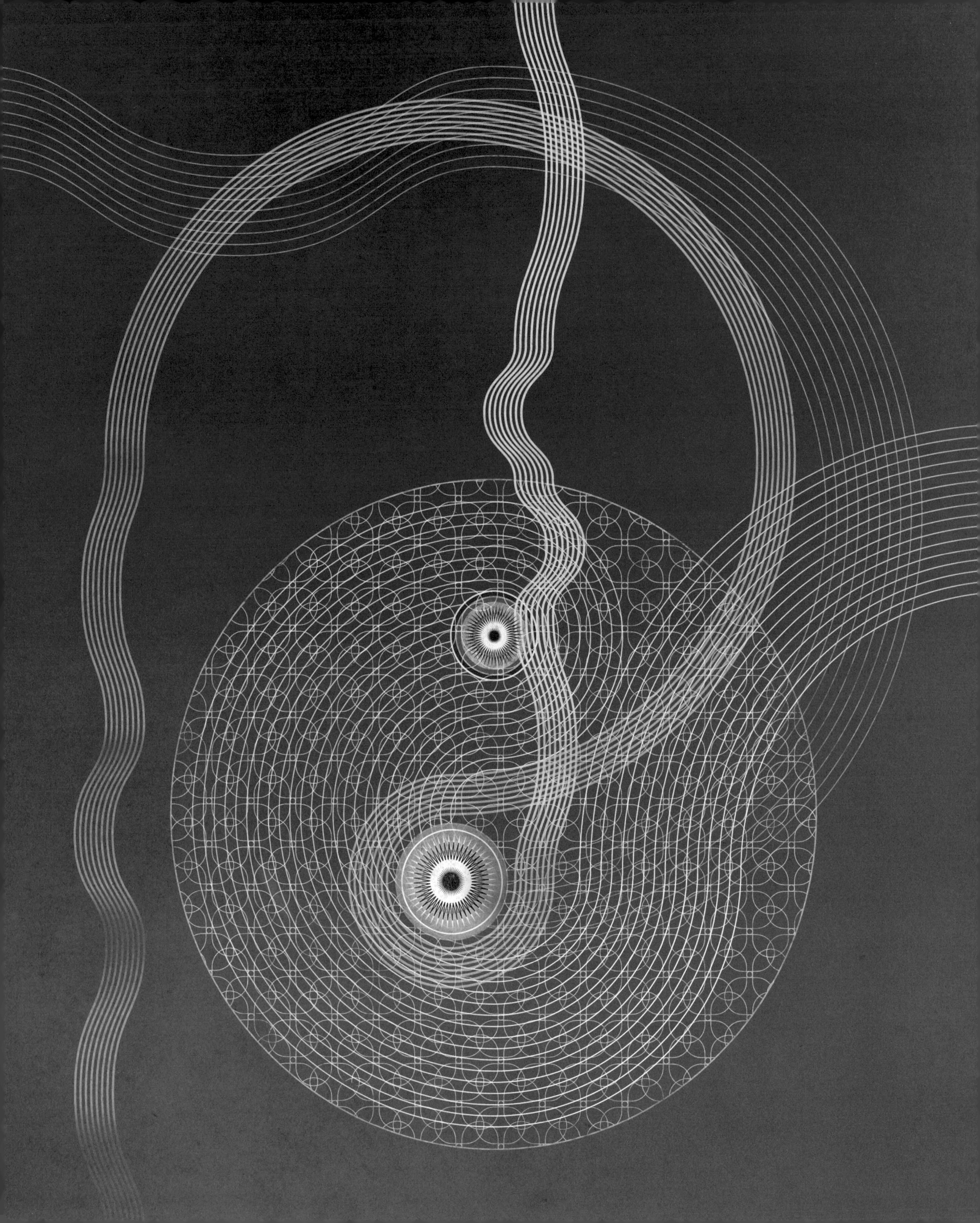

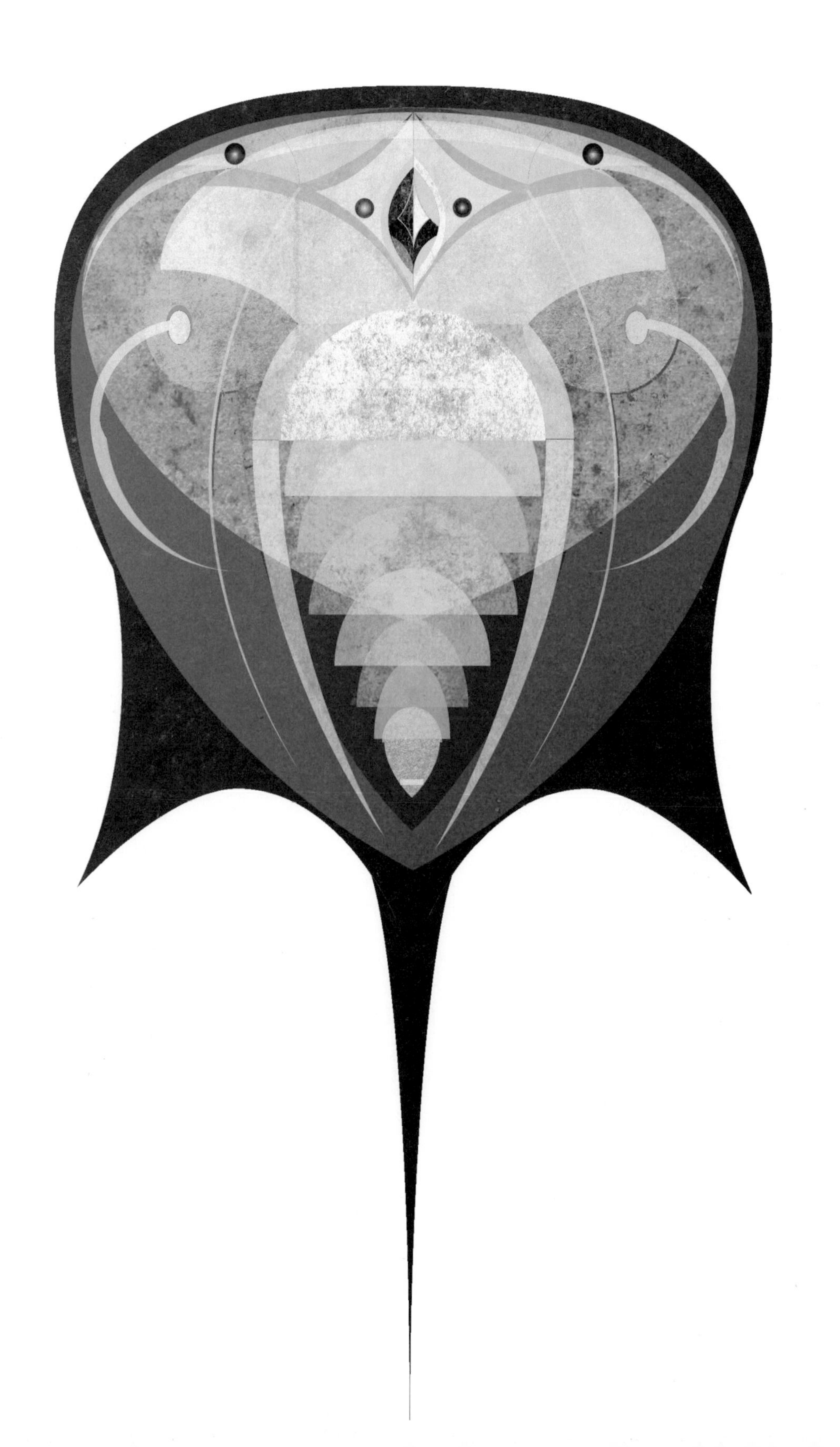

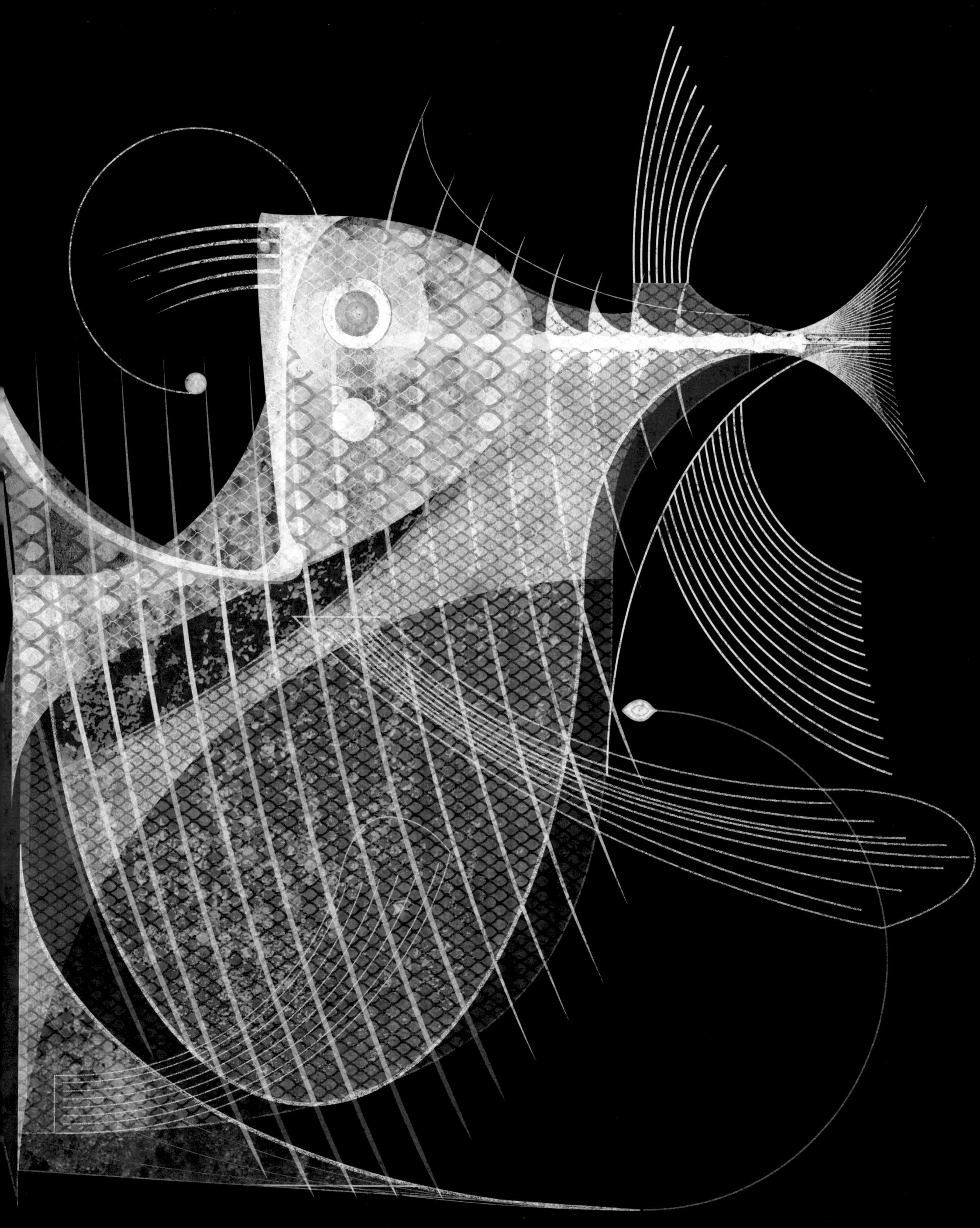

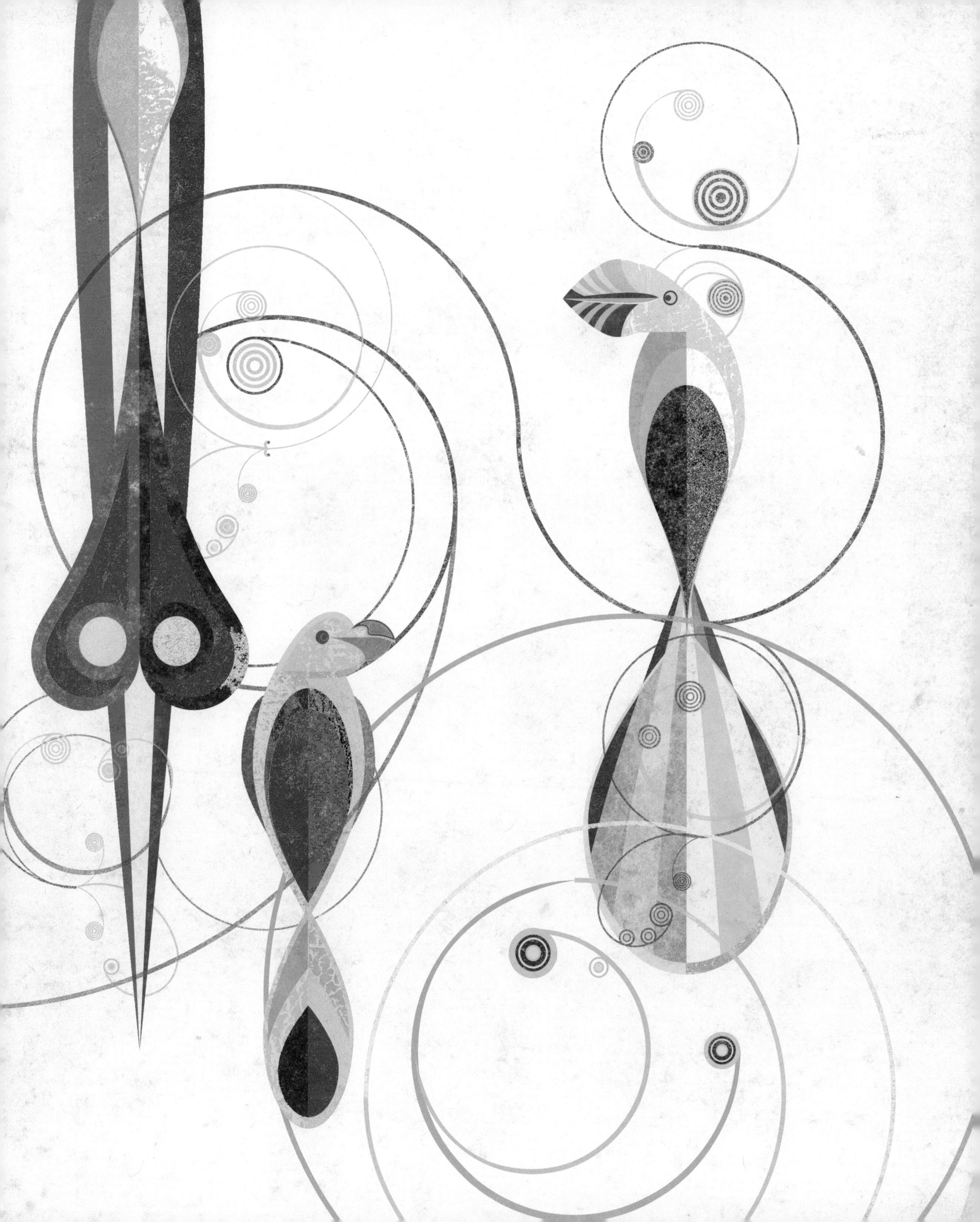

[24] And God said, "Let the land produce living creatures according to their kinds: livestock, creatures that move along the ground, and wild animals, each according to its kind." And it was so. [25] God made the wild animals according to their kinds, the livestock according to their kinds, and all the creatures that move along the ground according to their kinds. And God saw that it was good.

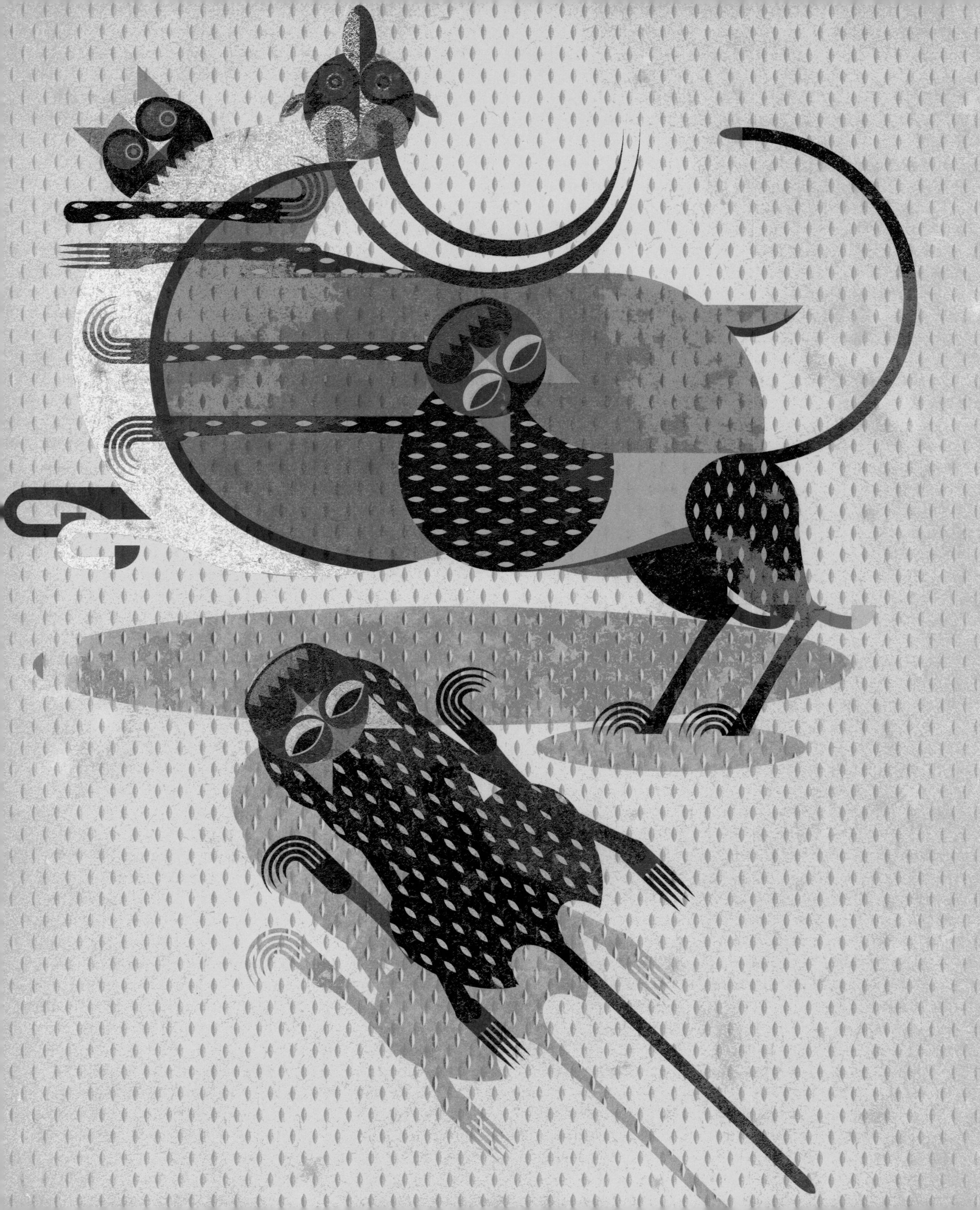

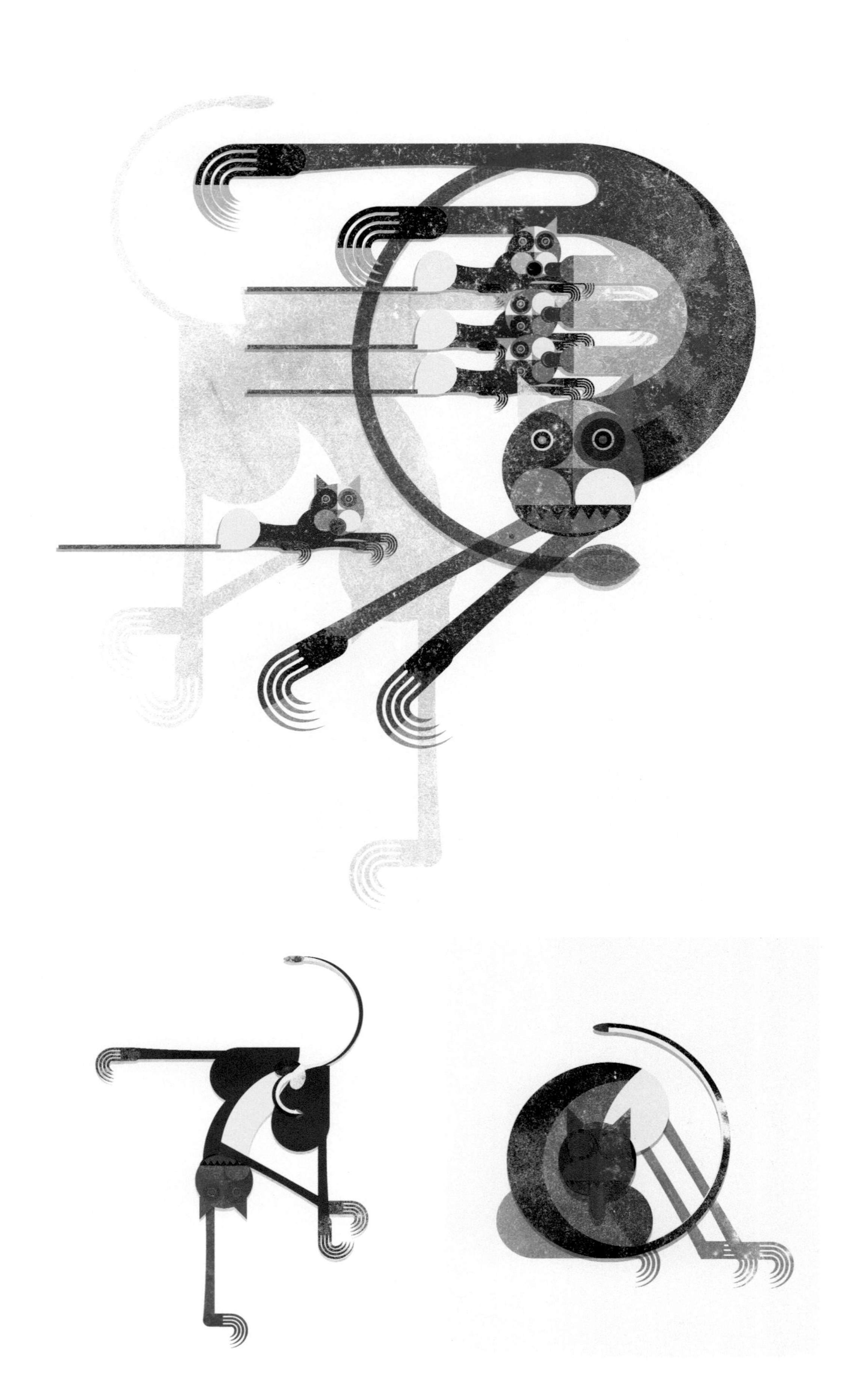

[26] Then God said, "Let us make man in our image, in our likeness, and let them rule over the fish of the sea and the birds of the air, over the livestock, over all the earth, and over all the creatures that move along the ground." [27] So God created man in his own image, in the image of God he created him; male and female he created them. [28] God blessed them and said to them, "Be fruitful and increase in number; fill the earth and subdue it. Rule over the fish of the sea and the birds of the air and over every living creature that moves on the ground."

[29] Then God said, "I give you every seed-bearing plant on the face of the whole earth and every tree that has fruit with seed in it. They will be yours for food. [30] And to all the beasts of the earth and all the birds of the air and all the creatures that move on the ground – everything that has the breath of life in it – I give every green plant for food." And it was so.

[31] God saw all that he had made, and it was very good. And there was evening, and there was morning – the sixth day.

[1] Thus the heavens and the earth were completed in all their vast array. [2] By the seventh day God had finished the work he had been doing; so on the seventh day he rested from all his work. [3] And God blessed the seventh day and made it holy, because on it he rested from all the work of creating that he had done.

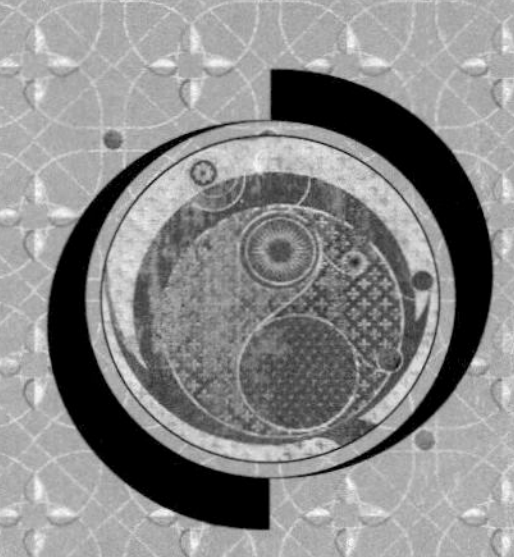

THE PARADISE

[4] This is the account of the heavens and the earth when they were created. When the LORD God made the earth and the heavens – [5] and no shrub of the field had yet appeared on the earth and no plant of the field had yet sprung up, for the LORD God had not sent rain on the earth and there was no man to work the ground, [6] but streams came up from the earth and watered the whole surface of the ground – [7] the LORD God formed the man from the dust of the ground and breathed into his nostrils the breath of life, and the man became a living being. [8] Now the LORD God had planted a garden in the east, in Eden; and there he put the man he had formed.

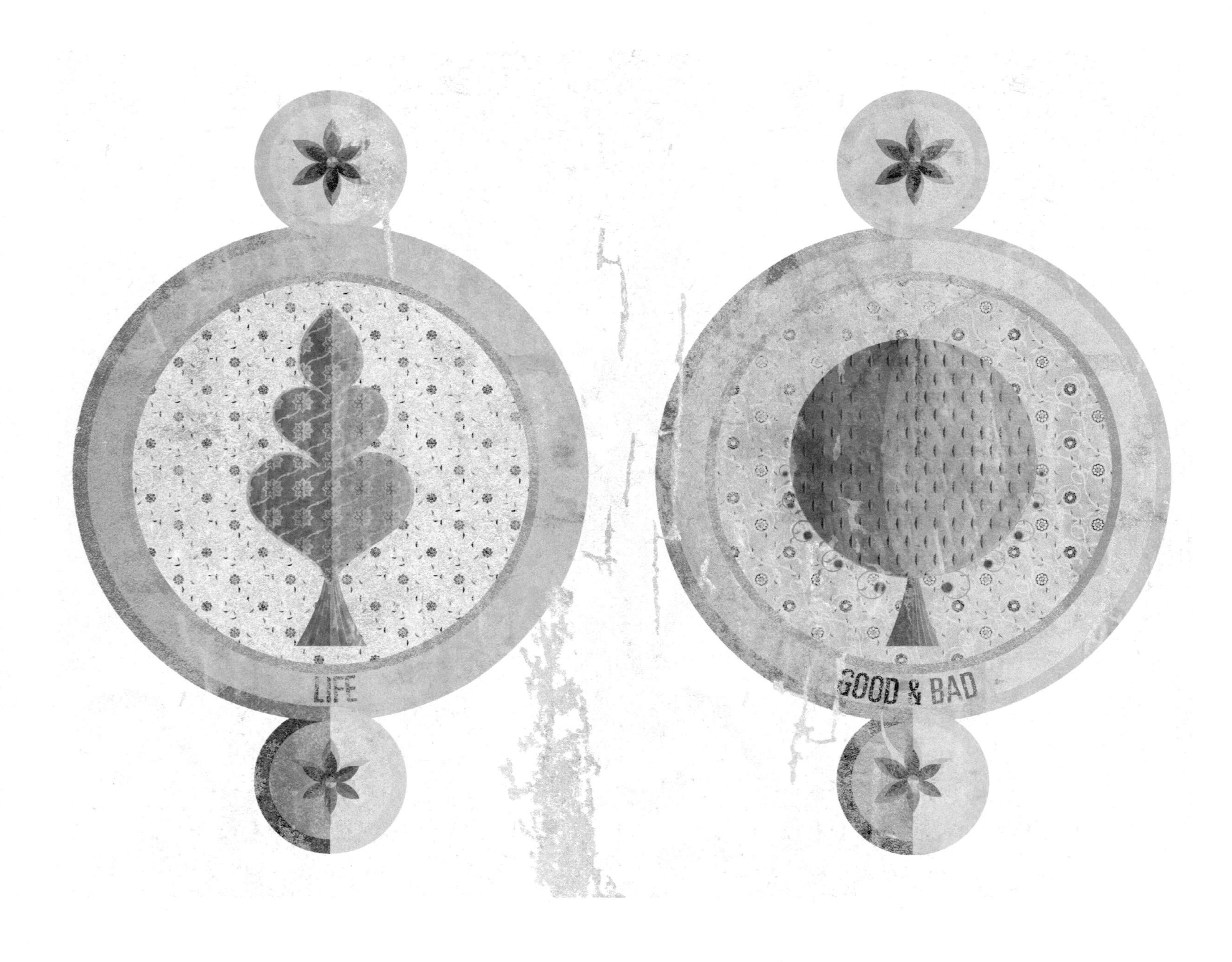

[9] And the LORD God made all kinds of trees grow out of the ground – trees that were pleasing to the eye and good for food. In the middle of the garden were the tree of life and the tree of the knowledge of good and evil.

[10] A river watering the garden flowed from Eden; from there it was separated into four headwaters. [11] The name of the first is the Pishon; it winds through the entire land of Havilah, where there is gold. [12] The gold of that land is good; aromatic resin and onyx are also there. [13] The

name of the second river is the Gihon; it winds through the entire land of Cush. [14] The name of the third river is the Tigris; it runs along the east side of Asshur. And the fourth river is the Euphrates.
[15] The LORD God took the man and put him in the Garden of Eden to work it and take care of it. [16] And the LORD God commanded the man, "You are free to eat from any tree in the garden; [17] but you must not eat from the tree of the knowledge of good and evil, for when you eat of it you will surely die."

N

[18] The LORD God said, "It is not good for the man to be alone. I will make a helper suitable for him."
[19] Now the LORD God had formed out of the ground all the beasts of the field and all the birds of the air. He brought them to the man to see what he would name them; and whatever the man called each living creature, that was its name. [20] So the man gave names to all the livestock, the birds of the air and all the beasts of the field.
But for Adam no suitable helper was found. [21] So the LORD God caused the man to fall into a deep sleep; and while he was sleeping, he took one of the man's ribs and closed up the place with flesh. [22] Then the LORD God made a woman from the rib he had taken out of the man, and he brought her to the man.
[23] The man said, "This is now bone of my bones and flesh of my flesh; she shall be called 'woman', for she was taken out of man."
[24] For this reason a man will leave his father and mother and be united to his wife, and they will become one flesh.
[25] The man and his wife were both naked, and they felt no shame.

THE FALL OF MAN

[1] Now the serpent was more crafty than any of the wild animals the LORD God had made. He said to the woman, "Did God really say, 'You must not eat from any tree in the garden'?"
[2] The woman said to the serpent, "We may eat fruit from the trees in the garden, [3] but God did say, 'You must not eat fruit from the tree that is in the middle of the garden, and you must not touch it, or you will die.' "
[4] "You will not surely die," the serpent said to the woman. [5] "For God knows that when you eat of it your eyes will be opened, and you will be like God, knowing good and evil."
[6] When the woman saw that the fruit of the tree was good for food and pleasing to the eye, and also desirable for gaining wisdom, she took some and ate it. She also gave some to her husband, who was with her, and he ate it.

[7] Then the eyes of both of them were opened, and they realized they were naked; so they sewed fig leaves together and made coverings for themselves. [8] Then the man and his wife heard the sound of the LORD God as he was walking in the garden in the cool of the day, and they hid from the LORD God among the trees of the garden. [9] But the LORD God called to the man, "Where are you?"

[10] He answered, "I heard you in the garden, and I was afraid because I was naked; so I hid."

[11] And he said, "Who told you that you were naked? Have you eaten from the tree that I commanded you not to eat from?"

[12] The man said, "The woman you put here with me – she gave me some fruit from the tree, and I ate it."

[13] Then the LORD God said to the woman, "What is this you have done?"

The woman said, "The serpent deceived me, and I ate."

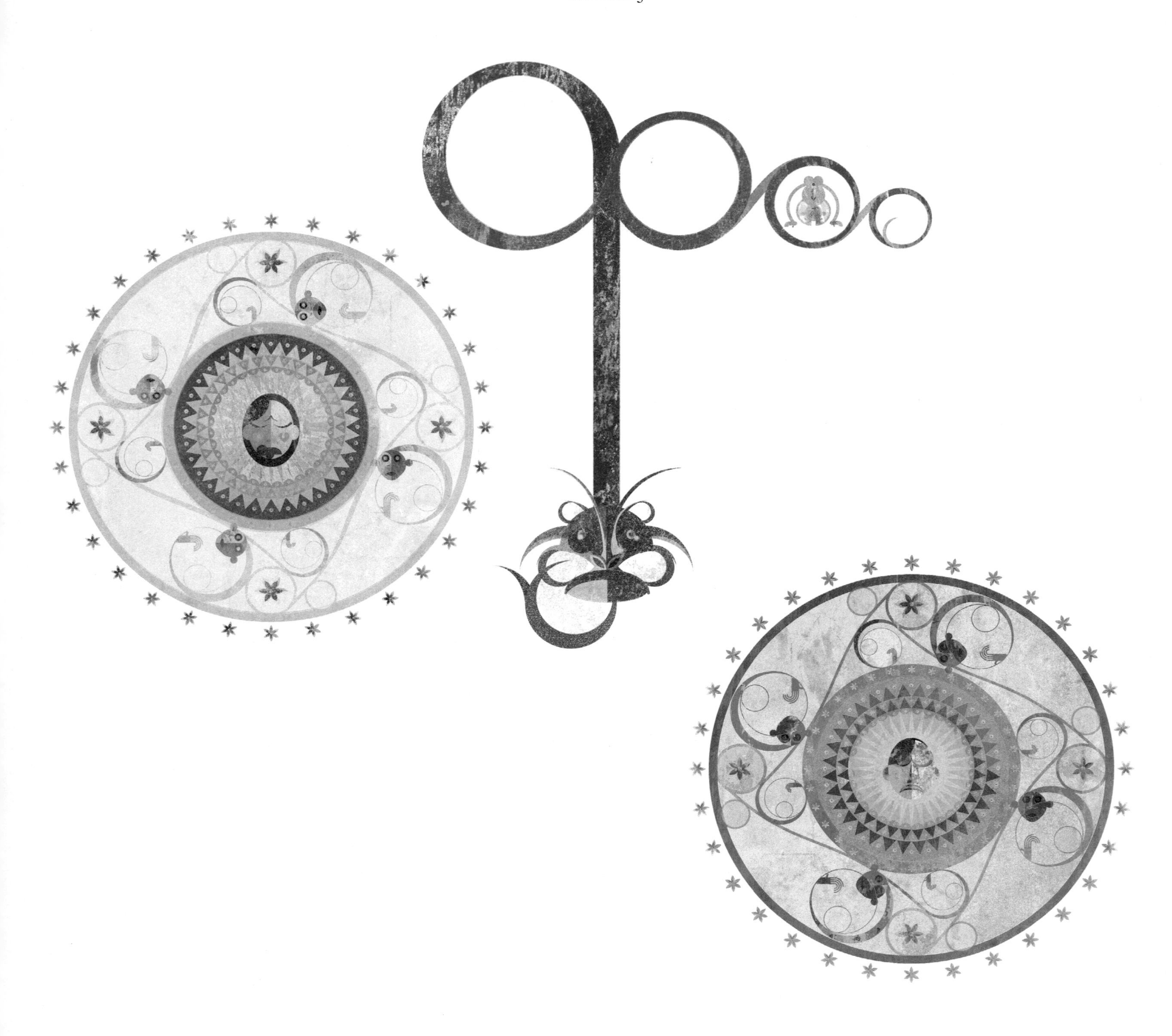

[14] So the LORD God said to the serpent, "Because you have done this, cursed are you above all the livestock and all the wild animals! You will crawl on your belly and you will eat dust all the days of your life. [15] And I will put enmity between you and the woman, and between your offspring and hers; he will crush your head, and you will strike his heel."
[16] To the woman he said, "I will greatly increase your pains in childbearing; with pain you will give birth to children. Your desire will be for your husband, and he will rule over you."

[17] To Adam he said, "Because you listened to your wife and ate from the tree about which I commanded you, 'You must not eat of it,' cursed is the ground because of you; through painful toil you will eat of it all the days of your life. [18] It will produce thorns and thistles for you, and you will eat the plants of the field. [19] By the sweat of your brow you will eat your food until you return to the ground, since from it you were taken; for dust you are and to dust you will return."

[20] Adam named his wife Eve, because she would become the mother of all the living. [21] The LORD God made garments of skin for Adam and his wife and clothed them. [22] And the LORD God said, "The man has now become like one of us, knowing good and evil. He must not be allowed to reach out his hand and take also from the tree of life and eat, and live forever." [23] So the LORD God banished him from the Garden of Eden to work the ground from which he had been taken. [24] After he drove the man out, he placed on the east side of the Garden of Eden cherubim and a flaming sword flashing back and forth to guard the way to the tree of life.

CAIN AND ABEL

[1] Adam lay with his wife Eve, and she became pregnant and gave birth to Cain. She said, "With the help of the LORD I have brought forth a man." [2] Later she gave birth to his brother Abel.
Now Abel kept flocks, and Cain worked the soil. [3] In the course of time Cain brought some of the fruits of the soil as an offering to the LORD. [4] But Abel brought fat portions from some of the firstborn of his flock. The LORD looked with favor on Abel and his offering, [5] but on Cain and his offering he did not look with favor. So Cain was very angry, and his face was downcast.
[6] Then the LORD said to Cain, "Why are you angry? Why is your face downcast? [7] If you do what is right, will you not be accepted? But if you do not do what is right, sin is crouching at your door; it desires to have you, but you must master it."
[8] Now Cain said to his brother Abel, "Let's go out to the field." And while they were in the field, Cain attacked his brother Abel and killed him.
[9] Then the LORD said to Cain, "Where is your brother Abel?"
"I don't know," he replied. "Am I my brother's keeper?"
[10] The LORD said, "What have you done? Listen! Your brother's blood cries out to me from the ground. [11] Now you are under a curse and driven from the ground, which opened its mouth to receive your brother's blood from your hand. [12] When you work the ground, it will no longer yield its crops for you. You will be a restless wanderer on the earth."
[13] Cain said to the LORD, "My punishment is more than I can bear. [14] Today you are driving me from the land, and I will be hidden from your presence; I will be a restless wanderer on the earth, and whoever finds me will kill me."
[15] But the LORD said to him, "Not so; if anyone kills Cain, he will suffer vengeance seven times over." Then the LORD put a mark on Cain so that no one who found him would kill him. [16] So Cain went out from the LORD's presence and lived in the land of Nod, east of Eden.

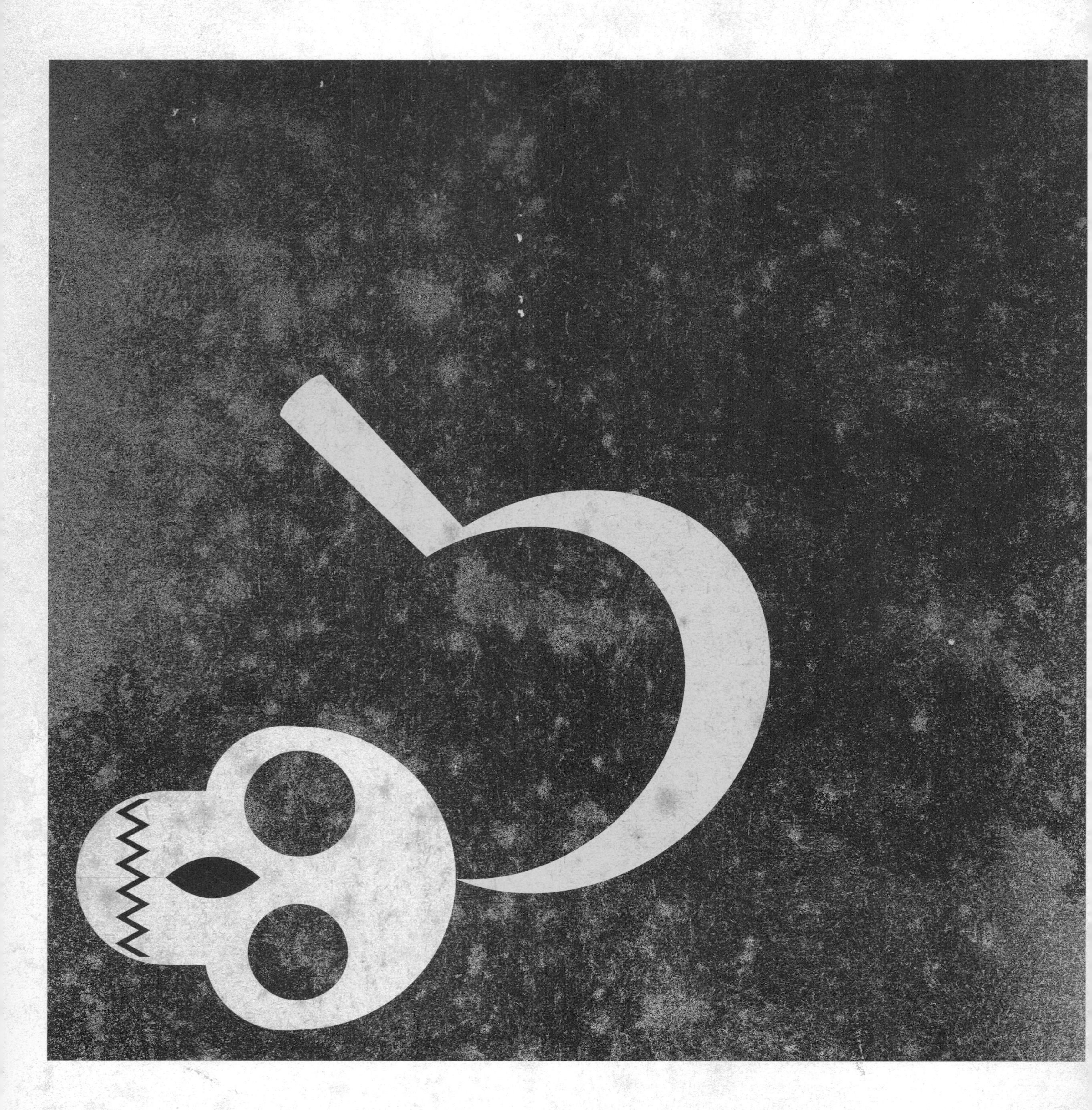

?
ABEL
!
WHAT HAVE YOU DONE
7
TIMES OVER

[17] Cain lay with his wife, and she became pregnant and gave birth to Enoch. Cain was then building a city, and he named it after his son Enoch. [18] To Enoch was born Irad, and Irad was the father of Mehujael, and Mehujael was the father of Methushael, and Methushael was the father of Lamech. [19] Lamech married two women, one named Adah and the other Zillah. [20] Adah gave birth to Jabal; he was the father of those who live in tents and raise livestock. [21] His brother's name was Jubal; he was the father of all who play the harp and flute. [22] Zillah also had a son, Tubal-Cain, who forged all kinds of tools out of bronze and iron. Tubal-Cain's sister was Naamah.

[23] Lamech said to his wives, "Adah and Zillah, listen to me; wives of Lamech, hear my words. I have killed a man for wounding me, a young man for injuring me. [24] If Cain is avenged seven times, then Lamech seventy-seven times."

[25] Adam lay with his wife again, and she gave birth to a son and named him Seth, saying, "God has granted me another child in place of Abel, since Cain killed him."

[26] Seth also had a son, and he named him Enosh. At that time men began to call on the name of the LORD.

FROM ADAM TO NOAH

[1] This is the written account of Adam's line. When God created man, he made him in the likeness of God. [2] He created them male and female and blessed them. And when they were created, he called them "man."

[3] When Adam had lived 130 years, he had a son in his own likeness, in his own image; and he named him Seth. [4] After Seth was born, Adam lived 800 years and had other sons and daughters. [5] Altogether, Adam lived 930 years, and then he died.

[6] When Seth had lived 105 years, he became the father of Enosh. [7] And after he became the father of Enosh, Seth lived 807 years and had other sons and daughters. [8] Altogether, Seth lived 912 years, and then he died.

[9] When Enosh had lived 90 years, he became the father of Kenan. [10] And after he became the father of Kenan, Enosh lived 815 years and had other sons and daughters. [11] Altogether, Enosh lived 905 years, and then he died.

[12] When Kenan had lived 70 years, he became the father of Mahalalel. [13] And after he became the father of Mahalalel, Kenan lived 840 years and had other sons and daughters. [14] Altogether, Kenan lived 910 years, and then he died.

[15] When Mahalalel had lived 65 years, he became the father of Jared. [16] And after he became the father of Jared, Mahalalel lived 830 years and had other sons and daughters. [17] Altogether, Mahalalel lived 895 years, and then he died.

[18] When Jared had lived 162 years, he became the father of Enoch. [19] And after he became the father of Enoch, Jared lived 800 years and had other sons and daughters. [20] Altogether, Jared lived 962 years, and then he died.

[21] When Enoch had lived 65 years, he became the father of Methuselah. [22] And after he became the father of Methuselah, Enoch walked with God 300 years and had other sons and daughters. [23] Altogether, Enoch lived 365 years. [24] Enoch walked with God; then he was no more, because God took him away.

[25] When Methuselah had lived 187 years, he became the father of Lamech. [26] And after he became the father of Lamech, Methuselah lived 782 years and had other sons and daughters. [27] Altogether, Methuselah lived 969 years, and then he died.

[28] When Lamech had lived 182 years, he had a son. [29] He named him Noah and said, "He will comfort us in the labor and painful toil of our hands caused by the ground the LORD has cursed." [30] After Noah was born, Lamech lived 595 years and had other sons and daughters. [31] Altogether, Lamech lived 777 years, and then he died.

[32] After Noah was 500 years old, he became the father of Shem, Ham and Japheth.

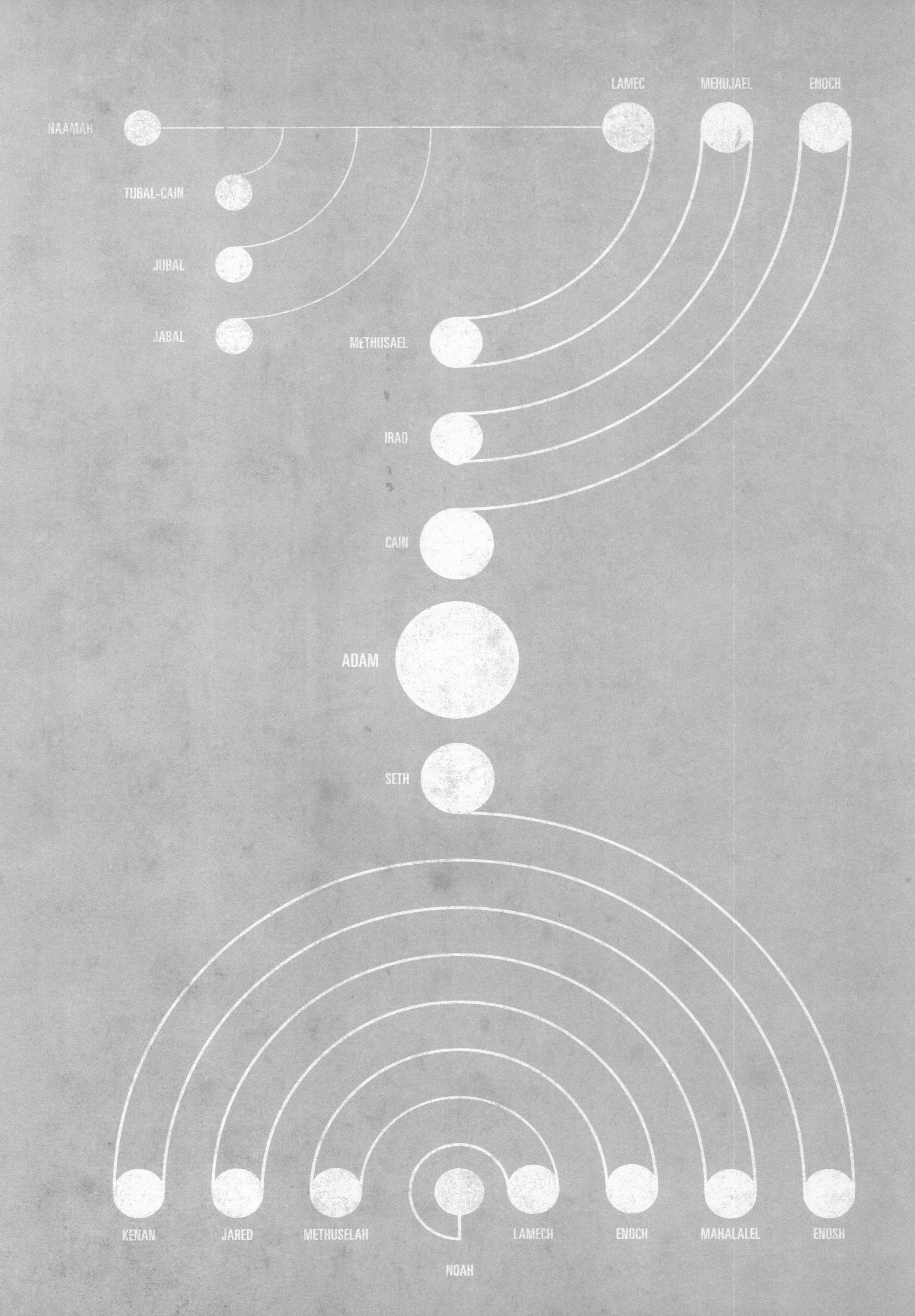
LAMEC
MEHUJAEL
ENOCH
NAAMAH
TUBAL-CAIN
JUBAL
JABAL
METHUSAEL
IRAD
CAIN
ADAM
SETH
KENAN
JARED
METHUSELAH
LAMECH
ENOCH
MAHALALEL
ENOSH
NOAH

THE FLOOD

[1] When men began to increase in number on the earth and daughters were born to them, [2] the sons of God saw that the daughters of men were beautiful, and they married any of them they chose. [3] Then the LORD said, "My Spirit will not contend with man forever, for he is mortal; his days will be a hundred and twenty years."

[4] The Nephilim were on the earth in those days – and also afterward – when the sons of God went to the daughters of men and had children by them. They were the heroes of old, men of renown.

[5] The LORD saw how great man's wickedness on the earth had become, and that every inclination of the thoughts of his heart was only evil all the time. [6] The LORD was grieved that he had made man on the earth, and his heart was filled with pain.

[7] So the LORD said, "I will wipe mankind, whom I have created, from the face of the earth – men and animals, and creatures that move along the ground, and birds of the air – for I am grieved that I have made them." [8] But Noah found favor in the eyes of the LORD.

[9] This is the account of Noah.

Noah was a righteous man, blameless among the people of his time, and he walked with God. [10] Noah had three sons: Shem, Ham and Japheth.

[11] Now the earth was corrupt in God's sight and was full of violence.

[12] God saw how corrupt the earth had become, for all the people on earth had corrupted their ways.

[13] So God said to Noah, "I am going to put an end to all people, for the earth is filled with violence because of them. I am surely going to destroy both them and the earth. [14] So make yourself an ark of cypress wood; make rooms in it and coat it with pitch inside and out. [15] This is how you are to build it: The ark is to be 450 feet long, 75 feet wide and 45 feet high. [16] Make a roof for it and finish the ark to within 18 inches of the top. Put a door in the side of the ark and make lower, middle and upper decks.

[17] I am going to bring floodwaters on the earth to destroy all life under the heavens, every creature that has the breath of life in it. Everything

on earth will perish. [18] But I will establish my covenant with you, and you will enter the ark – you and your sons and your wife and your sons' wives with you.
[19] You are to bring into the ark two of all living creatures, male and female, to keep them alive with you. [20] Two of every kind of bird, of every kind of animal and of every kind of creature that moves along the ground will come to you to be kept alive. [21] You are to take every kind of food that is to be eaten and store it away as food for you and for them."
[22] Noah did everything just as God commanded him.

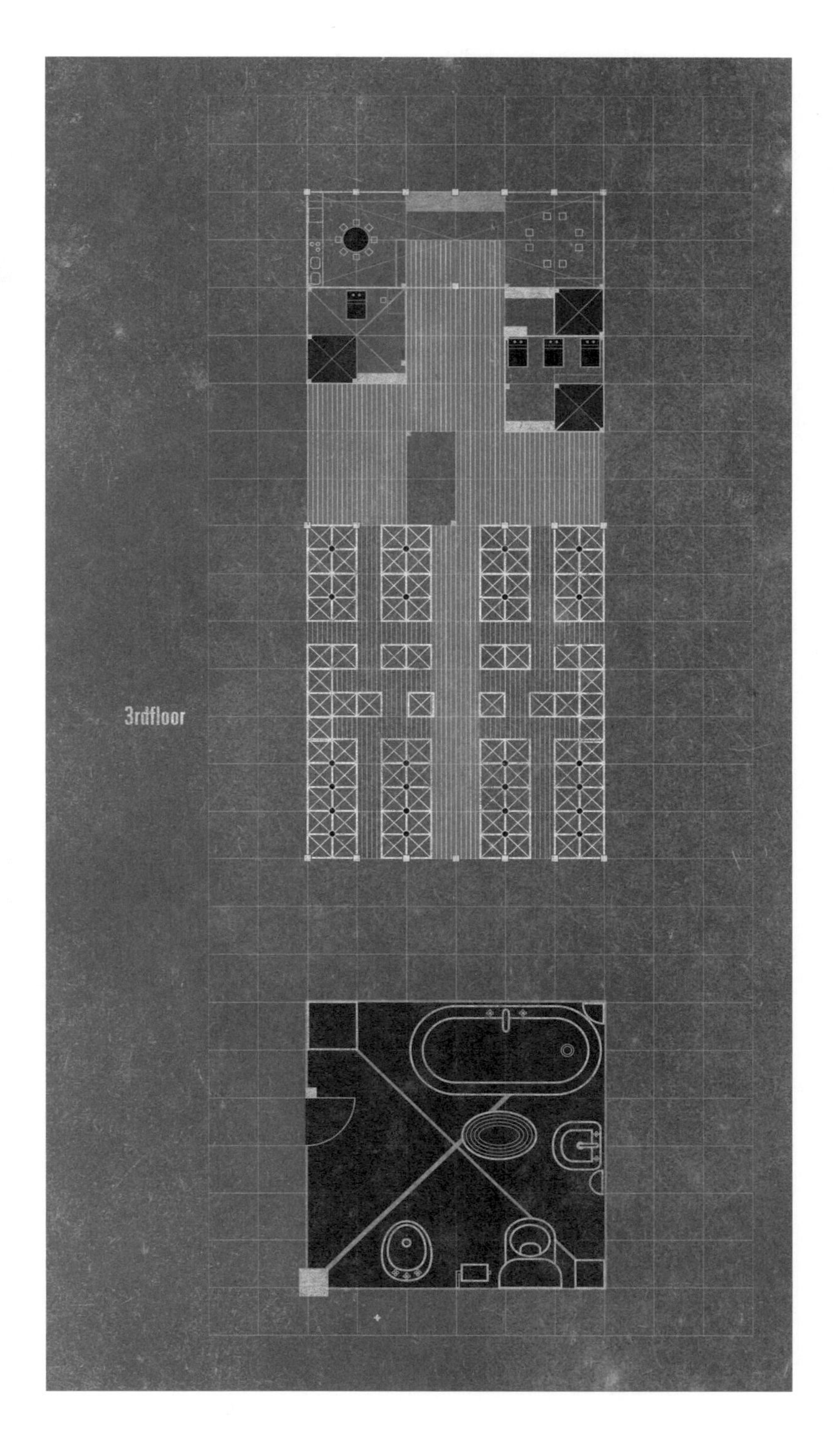

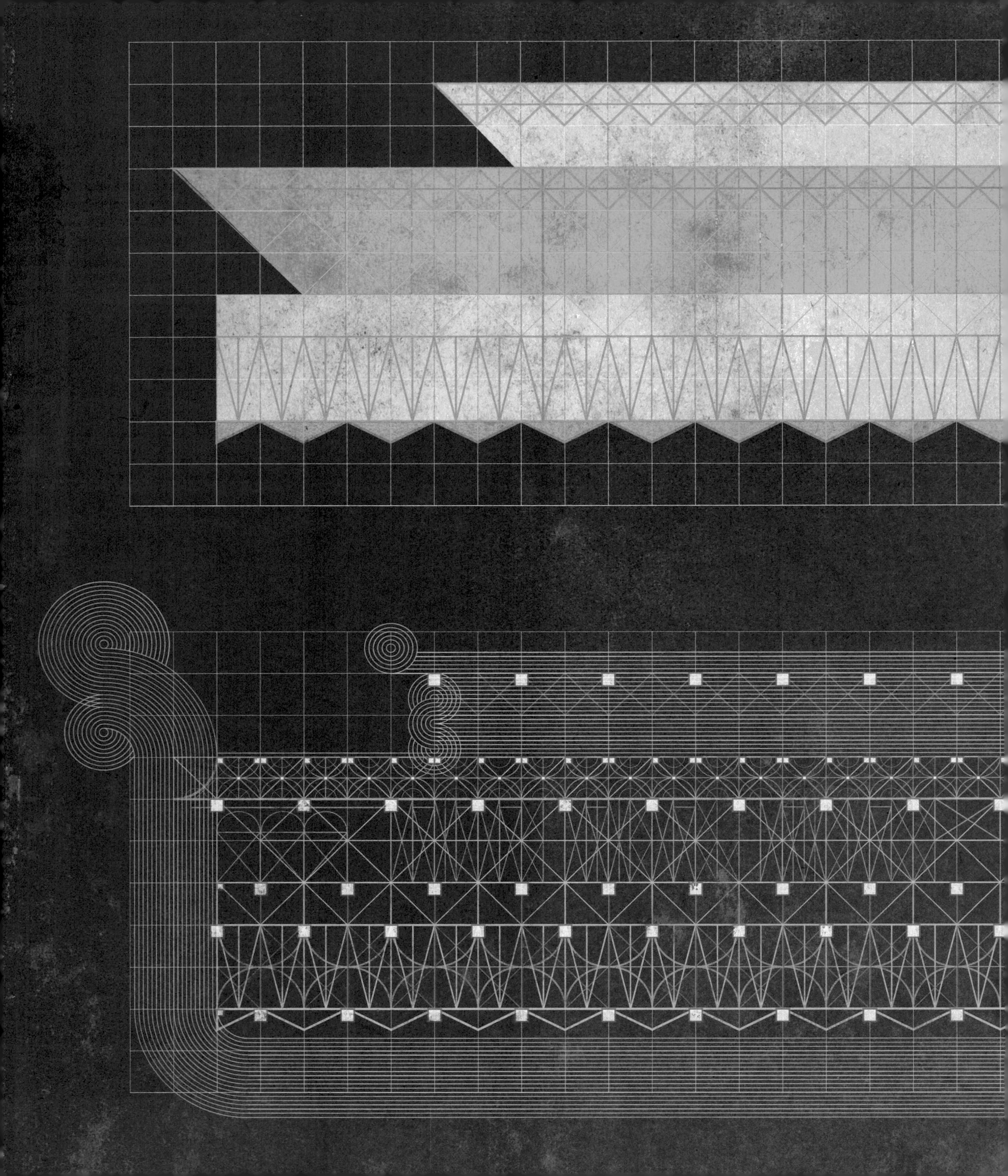

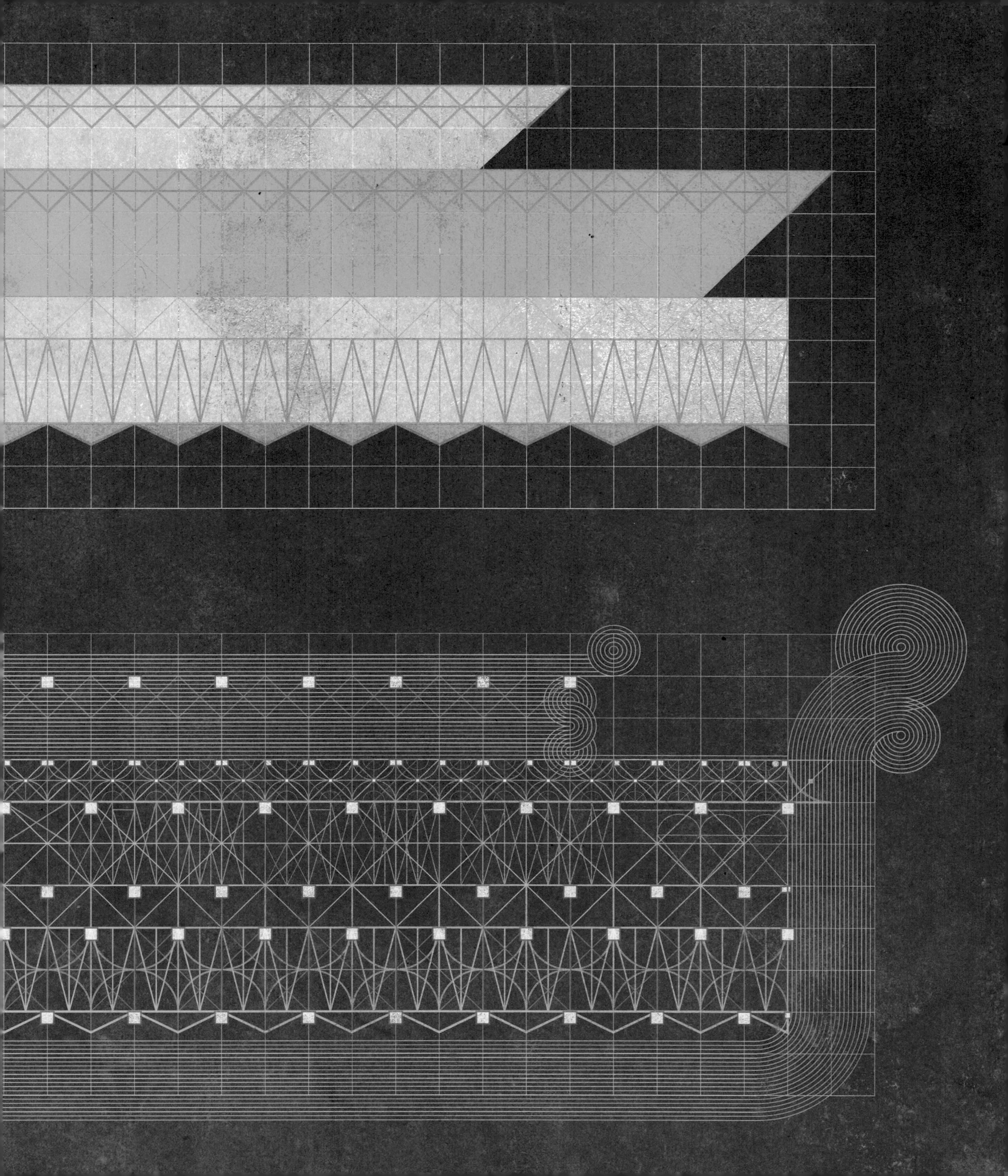

[1] The LORD then said to Noah, "Go into the ark, you and your whole family, because I have found you righteous in this generation. [2] Take with you seven of every kind of clean animal, a male and its mate, and two of every kind of unclean animal, a male and its mate, [3] and also seven of every kind of bird, male and female, to keep their various kinds alive throughout the earth. [4] Seven days from now I will send rain on the earth for forty days and forty nights, and I will wipe from the face of the earth every living creature I have made."

[5] And Noah did all that the LORD commanded him.

[6] Noah was six hundred years old when the floodwaters came on the earth. [7] And Noah and his sons and his wife and his sons' wives entered the ark to escape the waters of the flood. [8] Pairs of clean and unclean animals, of birds and of all creatures that move along the ground, [9] male and female, came to Noah and entered the ark, as God had commanded Noah. [10] And after the seven days the floodwaters came on the earth.

[11] In the six hundredth year of Noah's life, on the seventeenth day of the second month – on that day all the springs of the great deep burst forth, and the floodgates of the heavens were opened. [12] And rain fell on the earth forty days and forty nights.

[13] On that very day Noah and his sons, Shem, Ham and Japheth, together with his wife and the wives of his three sons, entered the ark. [14] They had with them every wild animal according to its kind, all livestock according to their kinds, every creature that moves along the ground according to its kind and every bird according to its kind, everything with wings. [15] Pairs of all creatures that have the breath of life in them came to Noah and entered the ark. [16] The animals going in were male and female of every living thing, as God had commanded Noah. Then the LORD shut him in.

[17] For forty days the flood kept coming on the earth, and as the waters increased they lifted the ark high above the earth. [18] The waters rose and increased greatly on the earth, and the ark floated on the surface of the water. [19] They rose greatly on the earth, and all the high mountains under the entire heavens were covered. [20] The waters rose and covered the mountains to a depth of more than twenty feet. [21] Every living thing that moved on the earth perished – birds, livestock, wild animals, all the creatures that swarm over the earth, and all mankind. [22] Everything on dry land that had the breath of life in its nostrils died. [23] Every living thing on the face of the earth was wiped out; men and animals and the creatures that move along the ground and the birds of the air were wiped from the earth. Only Noah was left, and those with him in the ark.
[24] The waters flooded the earth for a hundred and fifty days.

[1] But God remembered Noah and all the wild animals and the livestock that were with him in the ark, and he sent a wind over the earth, and the waters receded. [2] Now the springs of the deep and the floodgates of the heavens had been closed, and the rain had stopped falling from the sky. [3] The water receded steadily from the earth. At the end of the hundred and fifty days the water had gone down, [4] and on the seventeenth day of the seventh month the ark came to rest on the mountains of Ararat. [5] The waters continued to recede until the tenth month, and on the first day of the tenth month the tops of the mountains became visible.

[6] After forty days Noah opened the window he had made in the ark [7] and sent out a raven, and it kept flying back and forth until the water had dried up from the earth. [8] Then he sent out a dove to see if the water had receded from the surface of the ground. [9] But the dove could find no place to set its feet because there was water over all the surface of the earth; so it returned to Noah in the ark. He reached out his hand and took the dove and brought it back to himself in the ark. [10] He waited seven more days and again sent out the dove from the ark. [11] When the dove returned to him in the evening, there in its beak was a freshly plucked olive leaf! Then Noah knew that the water had receded from the earth. [12] He waited seven more days and sent the dove out again, but this time it did not return to him.

[13] By the first day of the first month of Noah's six hundred and first year, the water had dried up from the earth. Noah then removed the covering from the ark and saw that the surface of the ground was dry. [14] By the twenty-seventh day of the second month the earth was completely dry.

[15] Then God said to Noah, [16] "Come out of the ark, you and your wife and your sons and their wives. [17] Bring out every kind of living creature that is with you – the birds, the animals, and all the creatures that move along the ground – so they can multiply on the earth and be fruitful and increase in number upon it."

[18] So Noah came out, together with his sons and his wife and his sons' wives. [19] All the animals and all the creatures that move along the ground and all the birds – everything that moves on the earth – came out of the ark, one kind after another.
[20] Then Noah built an altar to the LORD and, taking some of all the clean animals and clean birds, he sacrificed burnt offerings on it. [21] The LORD smelled the pleasing aroma and said in his heart: "Never again will I curse the ground because of man, even though every inclination of his heart is evil from childhood. And never again will I destroy all living creatures, as I have done. [22] As long as the earth endures, seedtime and harvest, cold and heat, summer and winter, day and night will never cease."

GOD'S COVENANT WITH NOAH

[1] Then God blessed Noah and his sons, saying to them, "Be fruitful and increase in number and fill the earth. [2] The fear and dread of you will fall upon all the beasts of the earth and all the birds of the air, upon every creature that moves along the ground, and upon all the fish of the sea; they are given into your hands. [3] Everything that lives and moves will be food for you. Just as I gave you the green plants, I now give you everything.
[4] But you must not eat meat that has its lifeblood still in it. [5] And for your lifeblood I will surely demand an accounting. I will demand an accounting from every animal. And from each man, too, I will demand an accounting for the life of his fellow man.
[6] Whoever sheds the blood of man, by man shall his blood be shed; for in the image of God has God made man. [7] As for you, be fruitful and increase in number; multiply on the earth and increase upon it."
[8] Then God said to Noah and to his sons with him: [9] "I now establish my covenant with you and with your descendants after you [10] and with every living creature that was with you – the birds, the livestock and all the wild animals, all those that came out of the ark with you – every living creature on earth. [11] I establish my covenant with you: Never again will all life be cut off by the waters of a flood; never again will there be a flood to destroy the earth."
[12] And God said, "This is the sign of the covenant I am making between me and you and every living creature with you, a covenant for all generations to come: [13] I have set my rainbow in the clouds, and it will be the sign of the covenant between me and the earth. [14] Whenever I bring clouds over the earth and the rainbow appears in the clouds, [15] I will remember my covenant between me and you and all living creatures of every kind. Never again will the waters become a flood to destroy all life. [16] Whenever the rainbow appears in the clouds, I will see it and remember the everlasting covenant between God and all living creatures of every kind on the earth."
[17] So God said to Noah, "This is the sign of the covenant I have established between me and all life on the earth."

THE TABLE OF NATIONS

[1] This is the account of Shem, Ham and Japheth, Noah's sons, who themselves had sons after the flood.
The Japhethites. [2] The sons of Japheth: Gomer, Magog, Madai, Javan, Tubal, Meshech and Tiras. [3] The sons of Gomer: Ashkenaz, Riphath and Togarmah. [4] The sons of Javan: Elishah, Tarshish, the Kittim and the Rodanim. [5] From these the maritime peoples spread out into their territories by their clans within their nations, each with its own language.
The Hamites. [6] The sons of Ham: Cush, Mizraim, Put and Canaan. [7] The sons of Cush: Seba, Havilah, Sabtah, Raamah and Sabteca. The sons of Raamah: Sheba and Dedan. [8] Cush was the father of Nimrod, who grew to be a mighty warrior on the earth. [9] He was a mighty hunter before the LORD; that is why it is said, 'Like Nimrod, a mighty hunter before the LORD.' [10] The first centers of his kingdom were Babylon, Erech, Akkad and Calneh, in Shinar. [11] From that land he went to Assyria, where he built Nineveh, Rehoboth Ir, Calah [12] and Resen, which is between Nineveh and Calah; that is the great city. [13] Mizraim was the father of the Ludites, Anamites, Lehabites, Naphtuhites, [14] Pathrusites, Casluhites – from whom the Philistines came – and Caphtorites. [15] Canaan was the father of Sidon his firstborn, and of the Hittites, [16] Jebusites, Amorites, Girgashites, [17] Hivites, Arkites, Sinites, [18] Arvadites, Zemarites and Hamathites. Later the Canaanite clans scattered [19] and the borders of Canaan reached from Sidon toward Gerar as far as Gaza, and then toward Sodom, Gomorrah, Admah and Zeboiim, as far as Lasha. [20] These are the sons of Ham by their clans and languages, in their territories and nations.
The Semites. [21] Sons were also born to Shem, whose older brother was Japheth; Shem was the ancestor of all the sons of Eber. [22] The sons of Shem: Elam, Asshur, Arphaxad, Lud and Aram. [23] The sons of Aram: Uz, Hul, Gether and Meshech.[24] Arphaxad was the father of Shelah, and Shelah the father of Eber. [25] Two sons were born to Eber: One was named Peleg, because in his time the earth was divided; his brother was named Joktan. [26] Joktan was the father of Almodad, Sheleph, Hazarmaveth, Jerah, [27] Hadoram, Uzal, Diklah, [28] Obal, Abimael, Sheba, [29] Ophir, Havilah and Jobab. All these were sons of Joktan. [30] The region where they lived stretched from Mesha toward Sephar, in the eastern hill country. [31] These are the sons of Shem by their clans and languages, in their territories and nations.
[32] These are the clans of Noah's sons, according to their lines of descent, within their nations. From these the nations spread out over the earth after the flood.

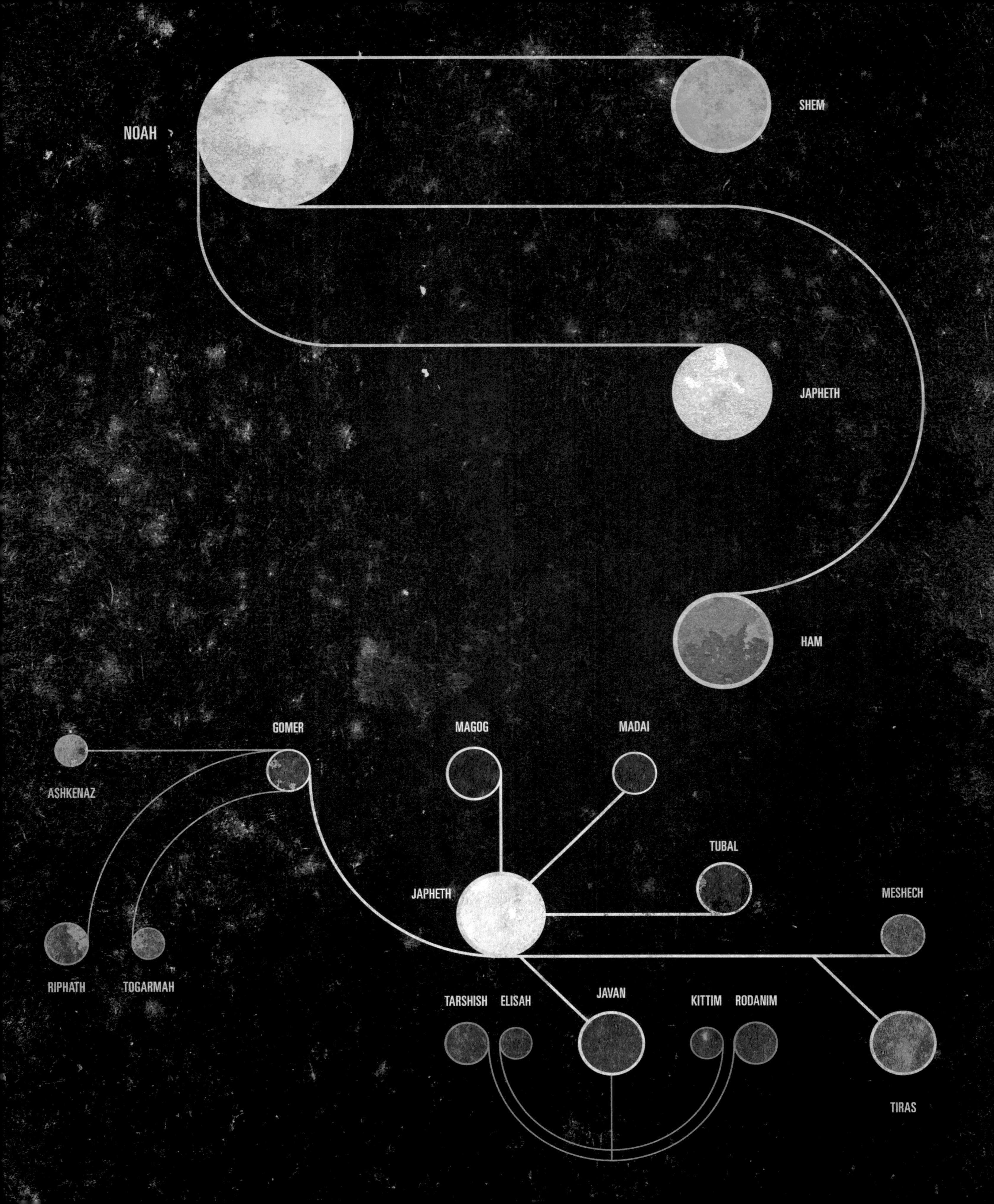
NOAH
SHEM
JAPHETH
HAM
GOMER
MAGOG
MADAI
ASHKENAZ
TUBAL
JAPHETH
MESHECH
RIPHATH
TOGARMAH
TARSHISH
ELISAH
JAVAN
KITTIM
RODANIM
TIRAS

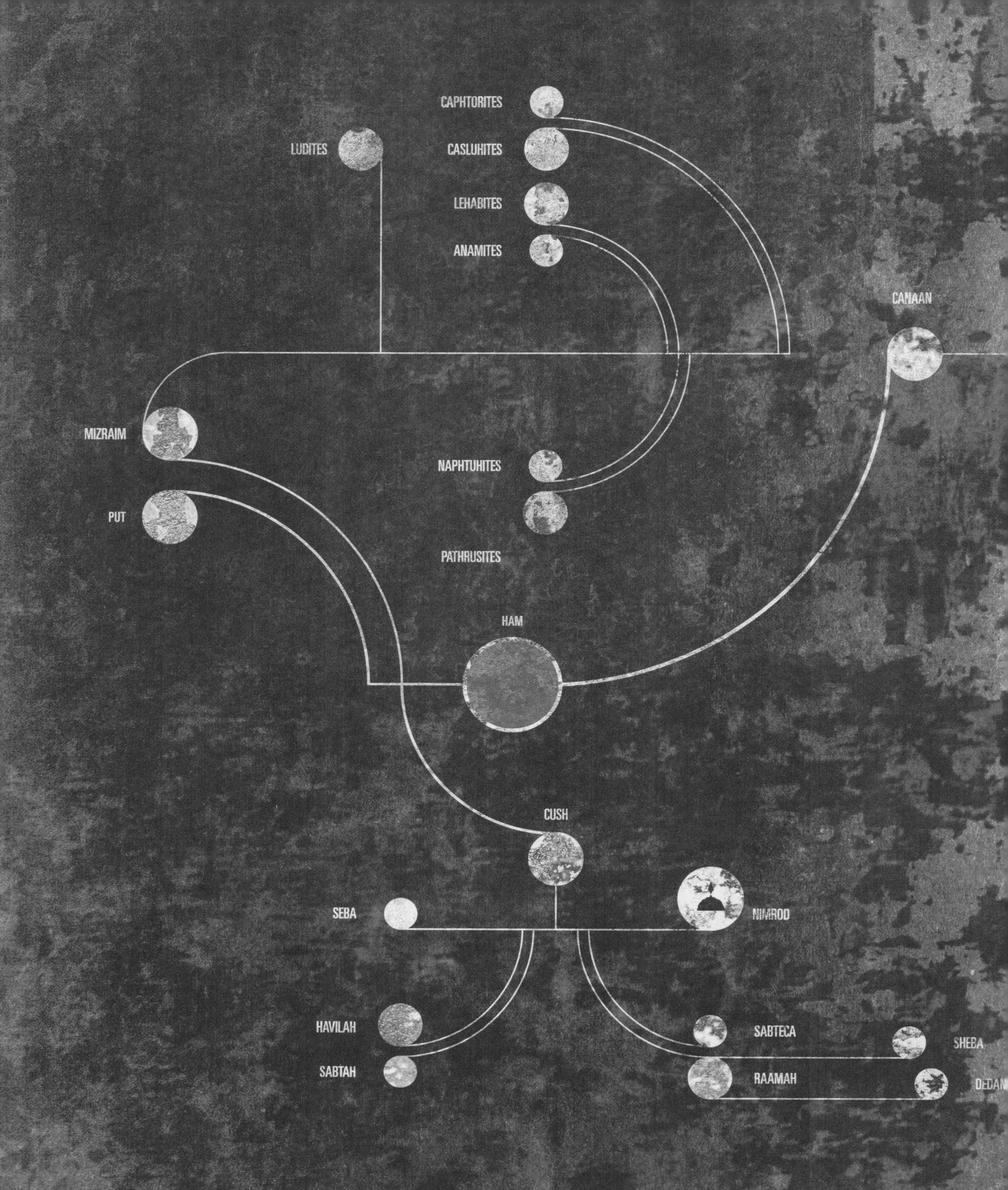
CAPHTORITES
LUDITES
CASLUHITES
LEHABITES
ANAMITES
CANAAN
MIZRAIM
NAPHTUHITES
PUT
PATHRUSITES
HAM
CUSH
SEBA
NIMROD
HAVILAH
SABTECA
SHEBA
SABTAH
RAAMAH
DEDAN

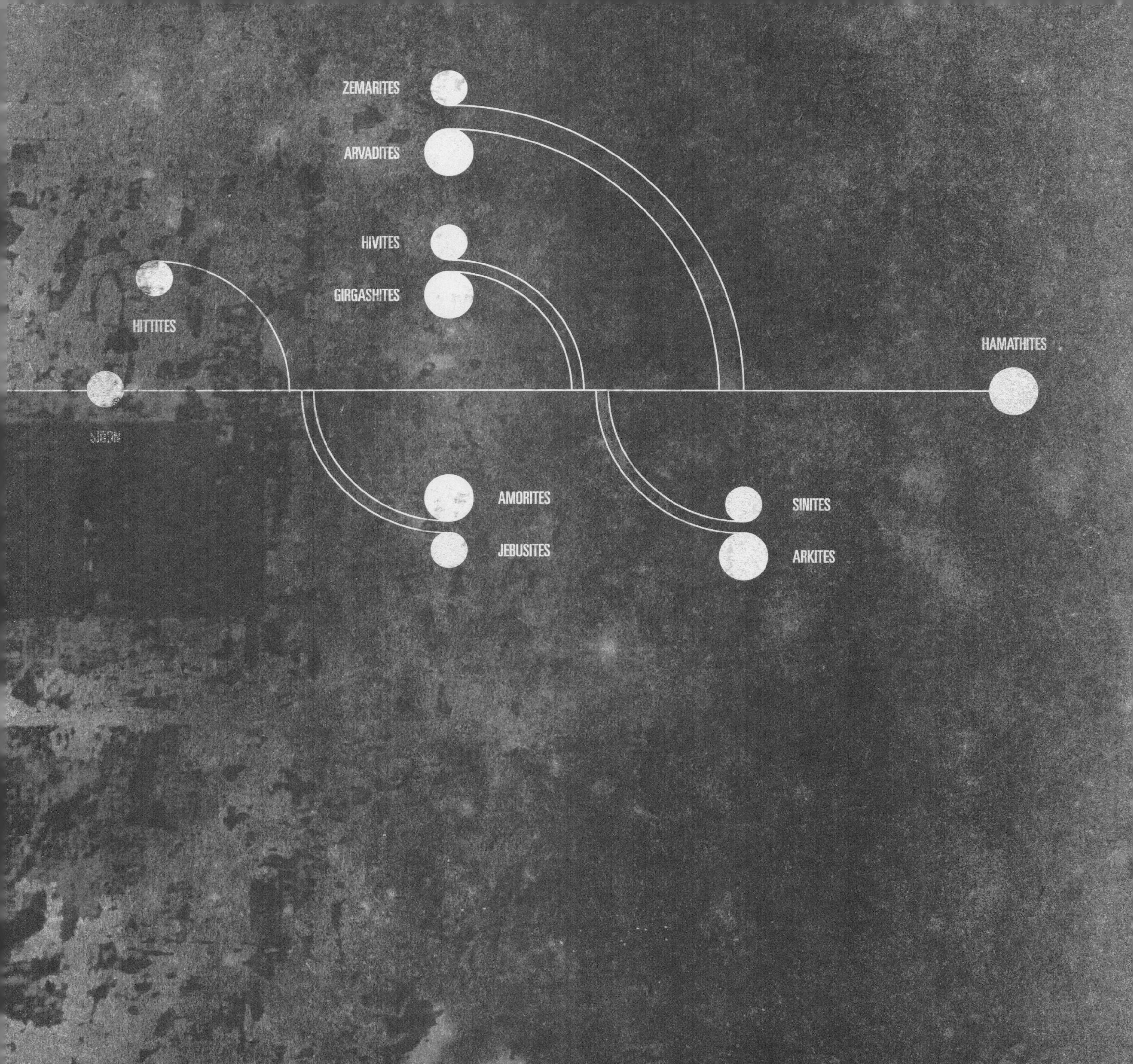
ZEMARITES
ARVADITES
HIVITES
GIRGASHITES
HITTITES
HAMATHITES
AMORITES
JEBUSITES
SINITES
ARKITES

THE TOWER OF BABEL

[1] Now the whole world had one language and a common speech. [2] As men moved eastward, they found a plain in Shinar and settled there. [3] They said to each other, "Come, let's make bricks and bake them thoroughly." They used brick instead of stone, and tar for mortar.

[4] Then they said, "Come, let us build ourselves a city, with a tower that reaches to the heavens, so that we may make a name for ourselves and not be scattered over the face of the whole earth."

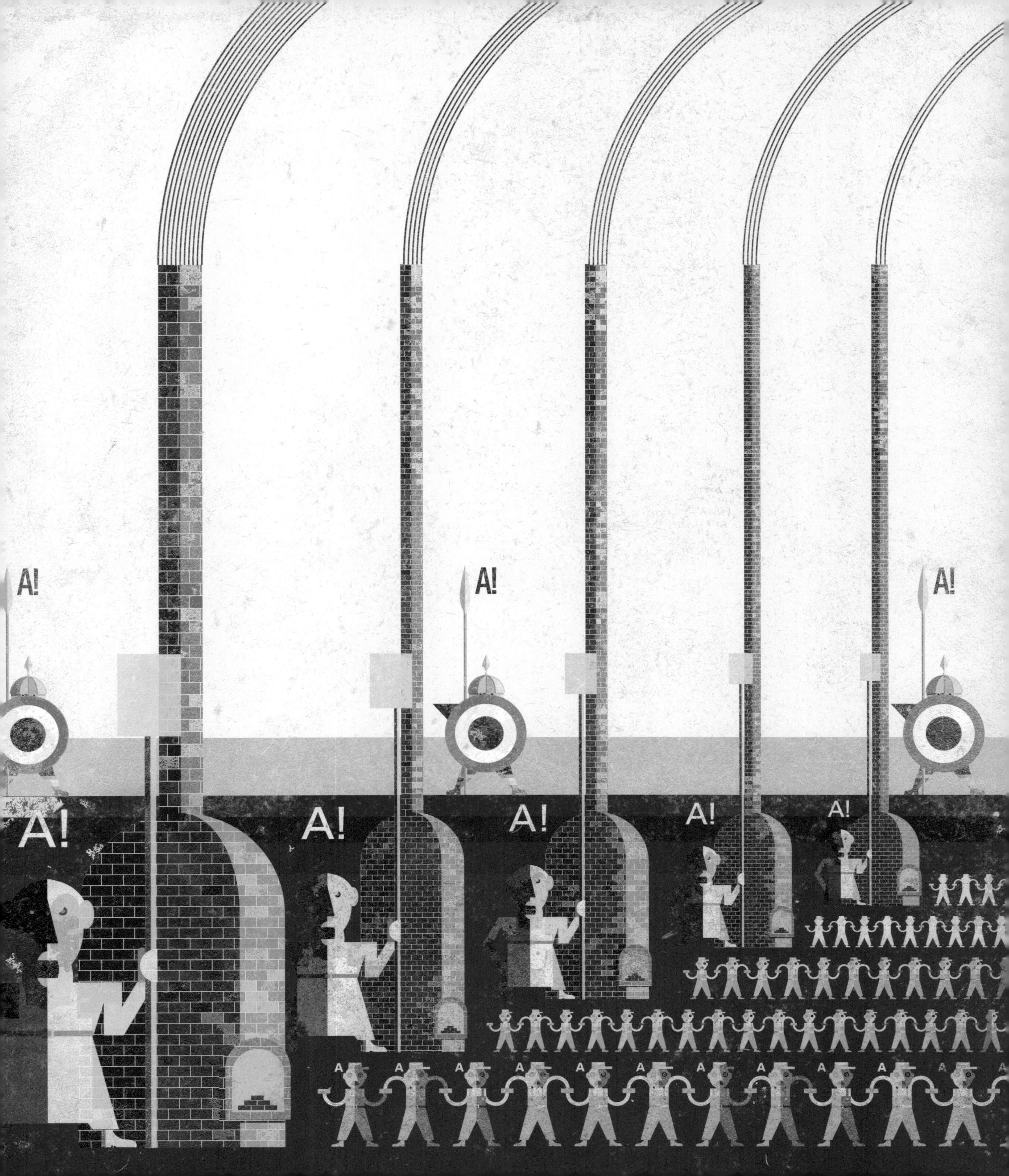

A!

A!

A!

A!

A!

A!

A!

A!

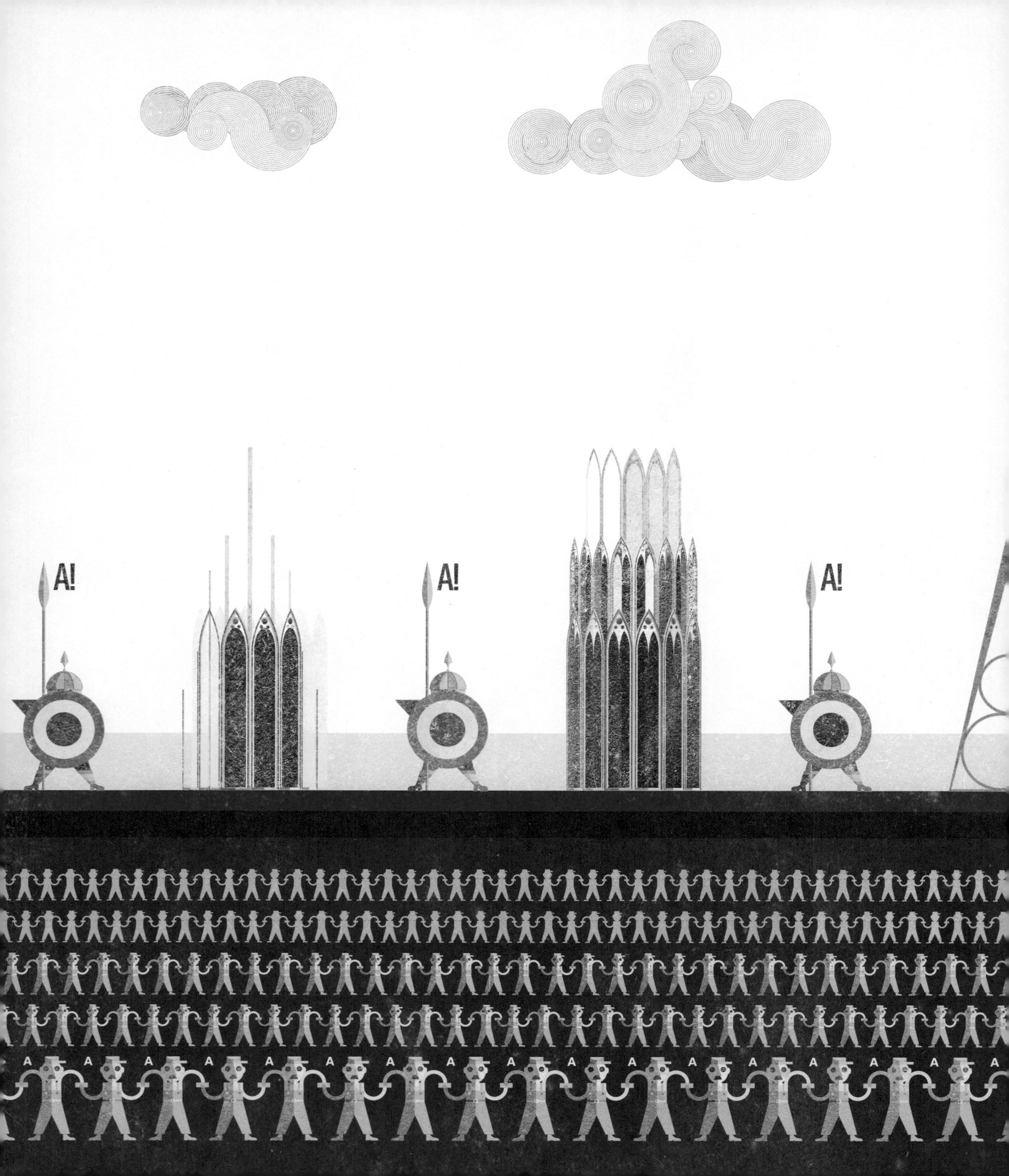
A!
A!
A!

A!
A!

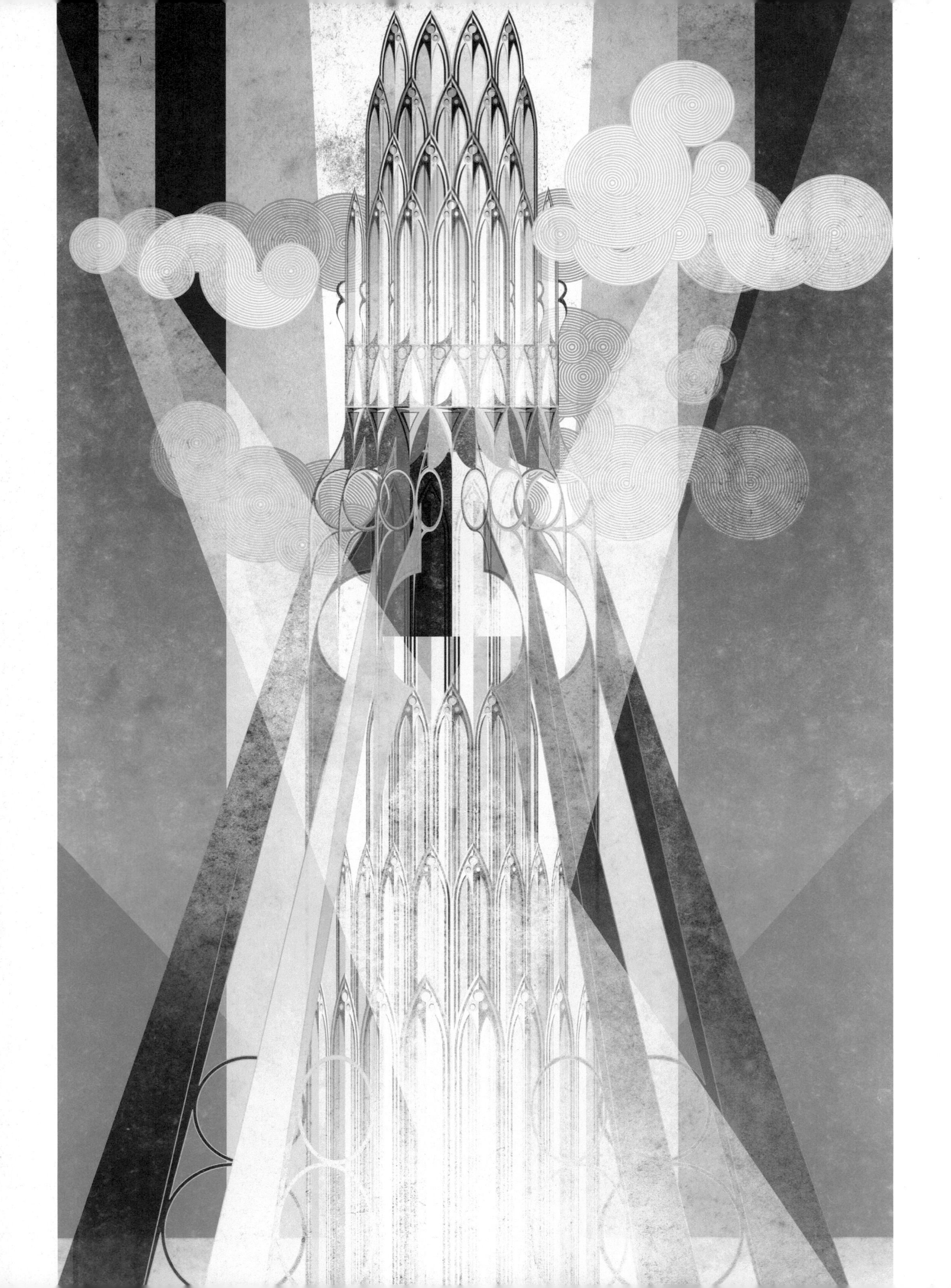

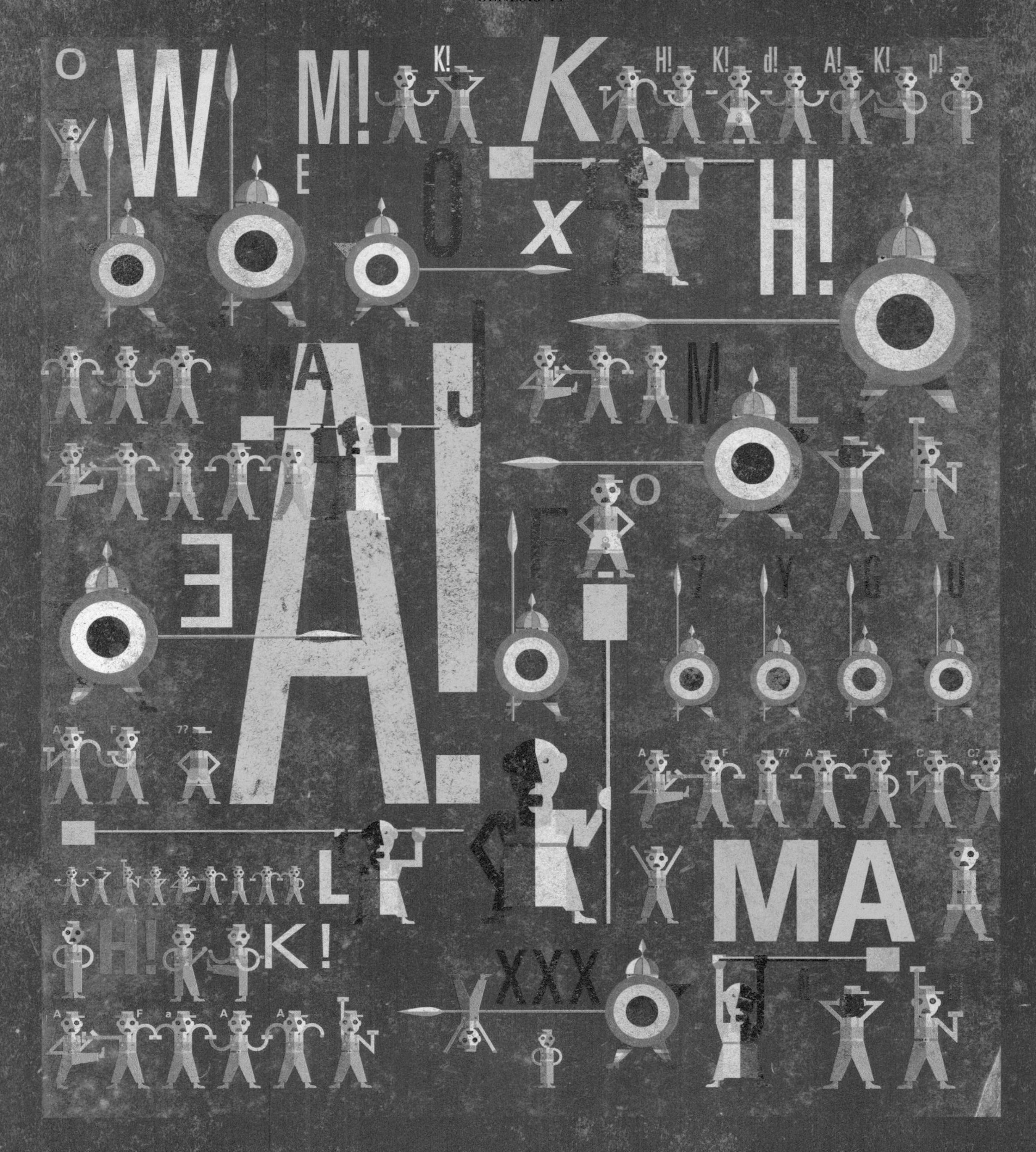

[5] But the LORD came down to see the city and the tower that the men were building. [6] The LORD said, "If as one people speaking the same language they have begun to do this, then nothing they plan to do will be impossible for them. [7] Come, let us go down and confuse their language so they will not understand each other."

[8] So the LORD scattered them from there over all the earth, and they stopped building the city. [9] That is why it was called Babel – because there the LORD confused the language of the whole world. From there the LORD scattered them over the face of the whole earth.

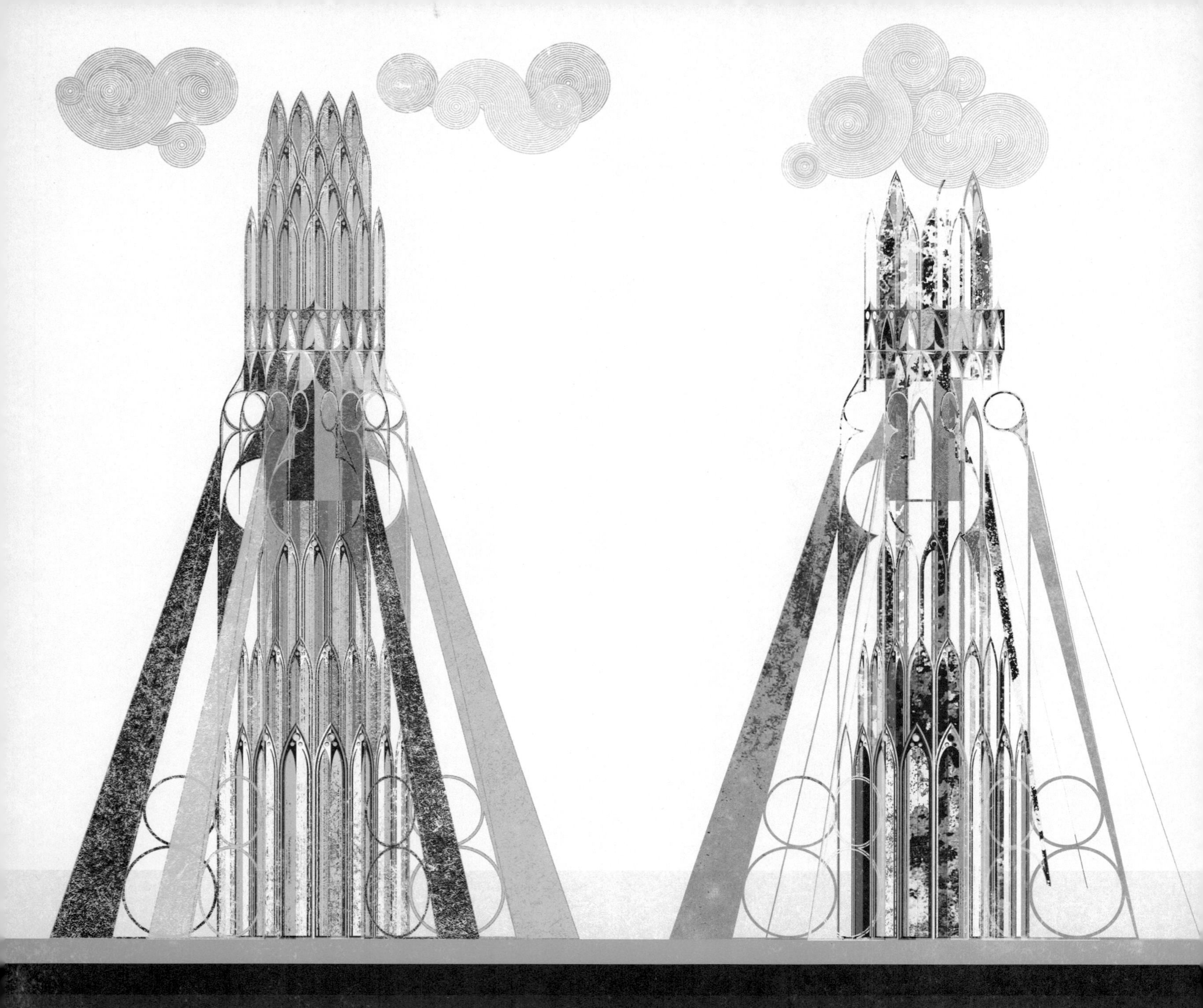

H! K!

K!

FROM SHEM TO ABRAM

[10] This is the account of Shem. Two years after the flood, when Shem was 100 years old, he became the father of Arphaxad. [11] And after he became the father of Arphaxad, Shem lived 500 years and had other sons and daughters. [12] When Arphaxad had lived 35 years, he became the father of Shelah. [13] And after he became the father of Shelah, Arphaxad lived 403 years and had other sons and daughters. [14] When Shelah had lived 30 years, he became the father of Eber. [15] And after he became the father of Eber, Shelah lived 403 years and had other sons and daughters. [16] When Eber had lived 34 years, he became the father of Peleg. [17] And after he became the father of Peleg, Eber lived 430 years and had other sons and daughters. [18] When Peleg had lived 30 years, he became the father of Reu. [19] And after he became the father of Reu, Peleg lived 209 years and had other sons and daughters. [20] When Reu had lived 32 years, he became the father of Serug. [21] And after he became the father of Serug, Reu lived 207 years and had other sons and daughters. [22] When Serug had lived 30 years, he became the father of Nahor. [23] And after he became the father of Nahor, Serug lived 200 years and had other sons and daughters. [24] When Nahor had lived 29 years, he became the father of Terah. [25] And after he became the father of Terah, Nahor lived 119 years and had other sons and daughters. [26] After Terah had lived 70 years, he became the father of Abram, Nahor and Haran.

[27] This is the account of Terah. Terah became the father of Abram, Nahor and Haran. And Haran became the father of Lot. [28] While his father Terah was still alive, Haran died in Ur of the Chaldeans, in the land of his birth. [29] Abram and Nahor both married. The name of Abram's wife was Sarai, and the name of Nahor's wife was Milcah; she was the daughter of Haran, the father of both Milcah and Iscah. [30] Now Sarai was barren; she had no children. [31] Terah took his son Abram, his grandson Lot son of Haran, and his daughter-in-law Sarai, the wife of his son Abram, and together they set out from Ur of the Chaldeans to go to Canaan. But when they came to Haran, they settled there. [32] Terah lived 205 years, and he died in Haran.

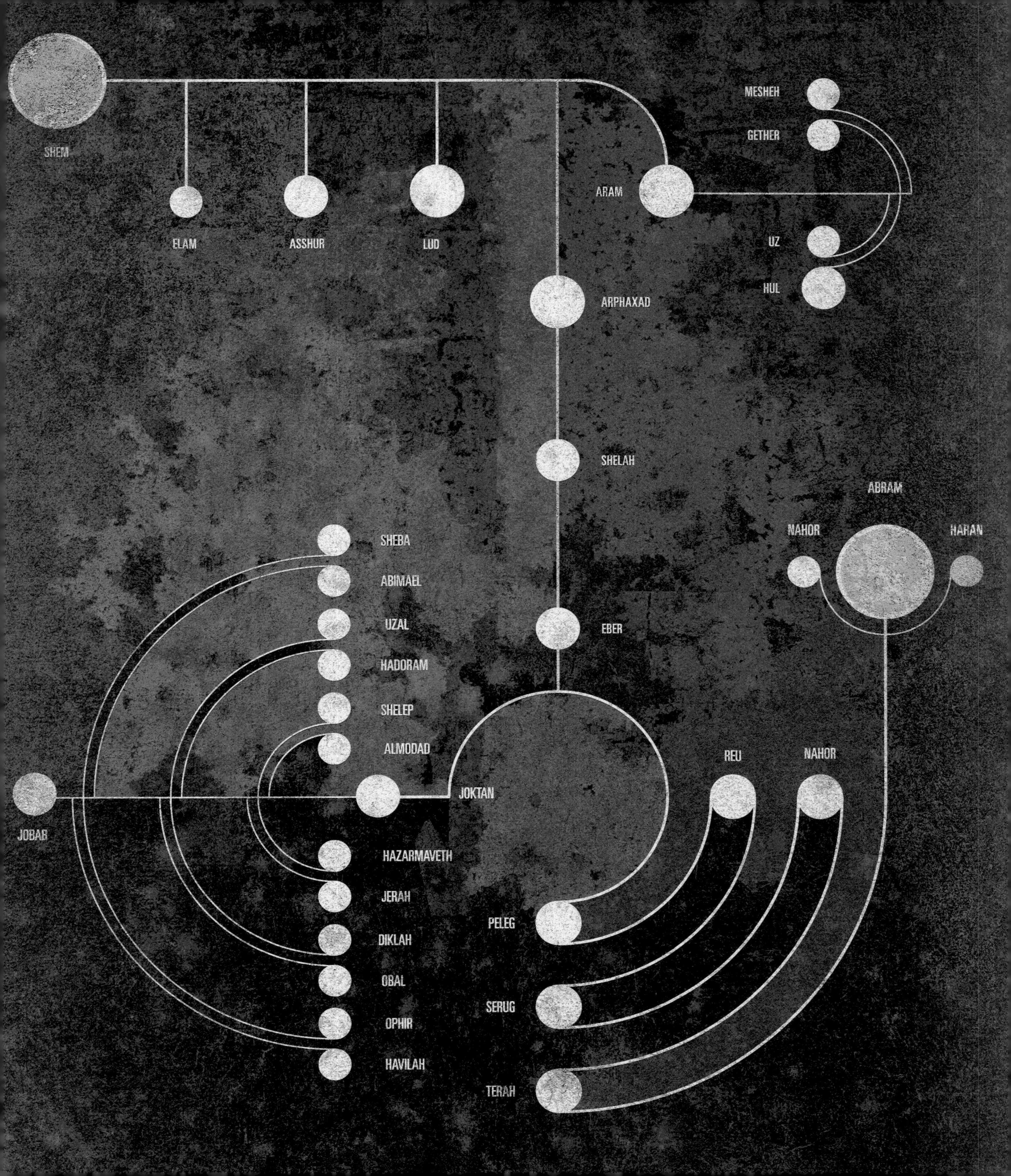
SHEM
ELAM
ASSHUR
LUD
ARAM
MESHEH
GETHER
UZ
HUL
ARPHAXAD
SHELAH
ABRAM
NAHOR
HARAN
SHEBA
ABIMAEL
UZAL
HADORAM
SHELEP
ALMODAD
EBER
JOBAB
JOKTAN
REU
NAHOR
HAZARMAVETH
JERAH
DIKLAH
OBAL
OPHIR
HAVILAH
PELEG
SERUG
TERAH

THE THREE VISITORS

[1] The LORD appeared to Abraham near the great trees of Mamre while he was sitting at the entrance to his tent in the heat of the day. [2] Abraham looked up and saw three men standing nearby. When he saw them, he hurried from the entrance of his tent to meet them and bowed low to the ground.

[3] He said, "If I have found favor in your eyes, my Lord, do not pass your servant by. [4] Let a little water be brought, and then you may all wash your feet and rest under this tree. [5] Let me get you something to eat, so you can be refreshed and then go on your way – now that you have come to your servant."

"Very well," they answered, "do as you say."

[6] So Abraham hurried into the tent to Sarah. "Quick," he said, "get three seahs of fine flour and knead it and bake some bread."

[7] Then he ran to the herd and selected a choice, tender calf and gave it to a servant, who hurried to prepare it. [8] He then brought some curds and milk and the calf that had been prepared, and set these before them. While they ate, he stood near them under a tree. [9] "Where is your wife Sarah?" they asked him.

"There, in the tent," he said.

[10] Then the LORD said, "I will surely return to you about this time next year, and Sarah your wife will have a son."

Now Sarah was listening at the entrance to the tent, which was behind him. [11] Abraham and Sarah were already old and well advanced in years, and Sarah was past the age of childbearing. [12] So Sarah laughed to herself as she thought, "After I am worn out and my master is old, will I now have this pleasure?"

[13] Then the LORD said to Abraham, "Why did Sarah laugh and say, 'Will I really have a child, now that I am old?' [14] Is anything too hard for the LORD? I will return to you at the appointed time next year and Sarah will have a son."

[15] Sarah was afraid, so she lied and said, "I did not laugh."

But he said, "Yes, you did laugh."

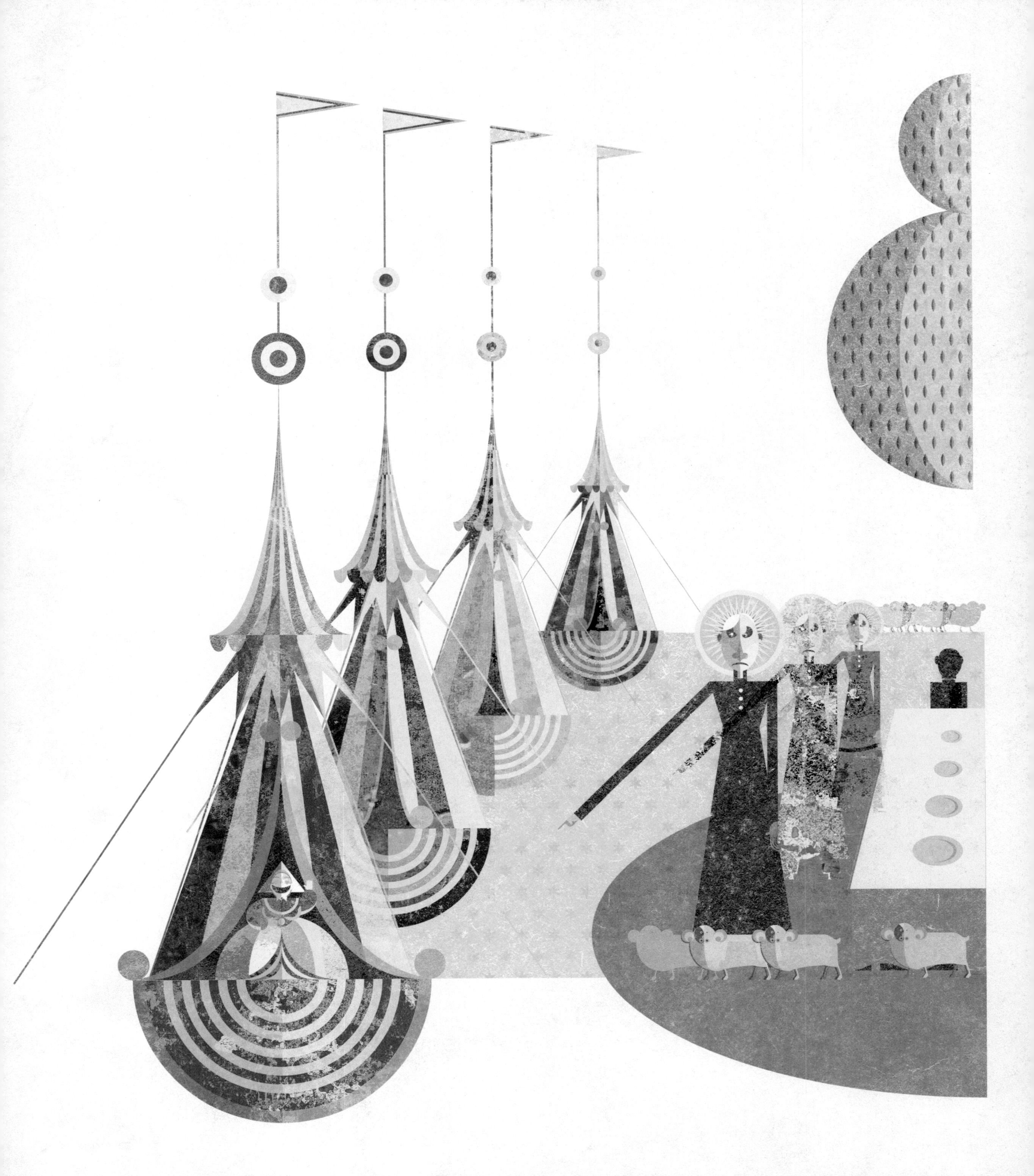

ABRAHAM PLEADS FOR SODOM

[16] When the men got up to leave, they looked down toward Sodom, and Abraham walked along with them to see them on their way.
[17] Then the LORD said, "Shall I hide from Abraham what I am about to do? [18] Abraham will surely become a great and powerful nation, and all nations on earth will be blessed through him. [19] For I have chosen him, so that he will direct his children and his household after him to keep the way of the LORD by doing what is right and just, so that the LORD will bring about for Abraham what he has promised him."
[20] Then the LORD said, "The outcry against Sodom and Gomorrah is so great and their sin so grievous [21] that I will go down and see if what they have done is as bad as the outcry that has reached me. If not, I will know."
[22] The men turned away and went toward Sodom, but Abraham remained standing before the LORD. [23] Then Abraham approached him and said: "Will you sweep away the righteous with the wicked? [24] What if there are fifty righteous people in the city? Will you really sweep it away and not spare the place for the sake of the fifty righteous people in it? [25] Far be it from you to do such a thing – to kill the righteous with the wicked, treating the righteous and the wicked alike. Far be it from you! Will not the Judge of all the earth do right?"
[26] The LORD said, "If I find fifty righteous people in the city of Sodom, I will spare the whole place for their sake."
[27] Then Abraham spoke up again: "Now that I have been so bold as to speak to the Lord, though I am nothing but dust and ashes, [28] what if the number of the righteous is five less than fifty? Will you destroy the whole city because of five people?"
"If I find forty-five there," he said, "I will not destroy it."
[29] Once again he spoke to him, "What if only forty are found there?"
He said, "For the sake of forty, I will not do it."
[30] Then he said, "May the Lord not be angry, but let me speak. What if only thirty can be found there?"
He answered, "I will not do it if I find thirty there."
[31] Abraham said, "Now that I have been so bold as to speak to the Lord, what if only twenty can be found there?"
He said, "For the sake of twenty, I will not destroy it."
[32] Then he said, "May the Lord not be angry, but let me speak just once more. What if only ten can be found there?"
He answered, "For the sake of ten, I will not destroy it."
[33] When the LORD had finished speaking with Abraham, he left, and Abraham returned home.

SODOM AND GOMORRAH DESTROYED

[1] The two angels arrived at Sodom in the evening, and Lot was sitting in the gateway of the city. When he saw them, he got up to meet them and bowed down with his face to the ground. [2] "My lords," he said, "please turn aside to your servant's house. You can wash your feet and spend the night and then go on your way early in the morning."
"No," they answered, "we will spend the night in the square."
[3] But he insisted so strongly that they did go with him and entered his house.

He prepared a meal for them, baking bread without yeast, and they ate. [4] Before they had gone to bed, all the men from every part of the city of Sodom – both young and old – surrounded the house.
[5] They called to Lot, "Where are the men who came to you tonight? Bring them out to us so that we can have sex with them."
[6] Lot went outside to meet them and shut the door behind him [7] and said, "No, my friends. Don't do this wicked thing. [8] Look, I have two daughters who have never slept with a man. Let me bring them out to you, and you can do what you like with them. But don't do anything to these men, for they have come under the protection of my roof."
[9] "Get out of our way," they replied. And they said, "This fellow came here as an alien, and now he wants to play the judge! We'll treat you worse than them."

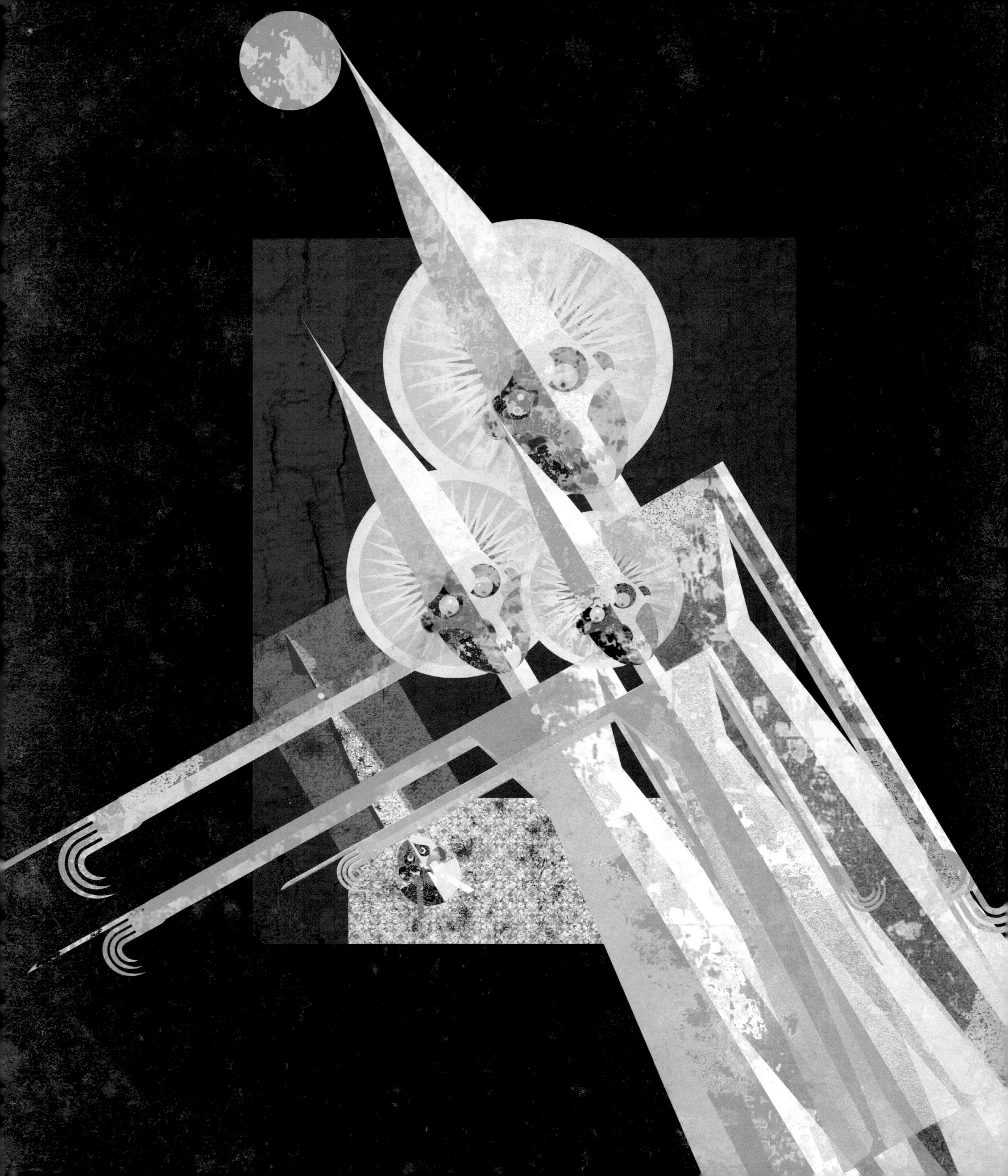

They kept bringing pressure on Lot and moved forward to break down the door. [10] But the men inside reached out and pulled Lot back into the house and shut the door. [11] Then they struck the men who were at the door of the house, young and old, with blindness so that they could not find the door.

[12] The two men said to Lot, "Do you have anyone else here – sons-in-law, sons or daughters, or anyone else in the city who belongs to you? Get them out of here, [13] because we are going to destroy this place. The outcry to the LORD against its people is so great that he has sent us to destroy it."

[14] So Lot went out and spoke to his sons-in-law, who were pledged to marry his daughters. He said, "Hurry and get out of this place, because the LORD is about to destroy the city!" But his sons-in-law thought he was joking.

[15] With the coming of dawn, the angels urged Lot, saying, "Hurry! Take your wife and your two daughters who are here, or you will be swept away when the city is punished."

[16] When he hesitated, the men grasped his hand and the hands of his wife and of his two daughters and led them safely out of the city, for the LORD was merciful to them. [17] As soon as they had brought them out, one of them said, "Flee for your lives! Don't look back, and don't stop anywhere in the plain! Flee to the mountains or you will be swept away!"

[18] But Lot said to them, "No, my lords, please! [19] Your servant has found favor in your eyes, and you have shown great kindness to me in sparing my life. But I can't flee to the mountains; this disaster will overtake me, and I'll die. [20] Look, here is a town near enough to run to, and it is small. Let me flee to it – it is very small, isn't it? Then my life will be spared."

[21] He said to him, "Very well, I will grant this request too; I will not overthrow the town you speak of. [22] But flee there quickly, because I cannot do anything until you reach it." That is why the town was called Zoar.

[23] By the time Lot reached Zoar, the sun had risen over the land. [24] Then the LORD rained down burning sulfur on Sodom and Gomorrah – from the LORD out of the heavens. [25] Thus he overthrew those cities and the entire plain, including all those living in the cities – and also the vegetation in the land. [26] But Lot's wife looked back, and she became a pillar of salt.

[27] Early the next morning Abraham got up and returned to the place where he had stood before the LORD. [28] He looked down toward Sodom and Gomorrah, toward all the land of the plain, and he saw dense smoke rising from the land, like smoke from a furnace.

[29] So when God destroyed the cities of the plain, he remembered Abraham, and he brought Lot out of the catastrophe that overthrew the cities where Lot had lived.

LOT AND HIS DAUGHTERS

[30] Lot and his two daughters left Zoar and settled in the mountains, for he was afraid to stay in Zoar. He and his two daughters lived in a cave. [31] One day the older daughter said to the younger, "Our father is old, and there is no man around here to lie with us, as is the custom all over the earth. [32] Let's get our father to drink wine and then lie with him and preserve our family line through our father."

[33] That night they got their father to drink wine, and the older daughter went in and lay with him. He was not aware of it when she lay down or when she got up.

[34] The next day the older daughter said to the younger, "Last night I lay

with my father. Let's get him to drink wine again tonight, and you go in and lie with him so we can preserve our family line through our father." [35] So they got their father to drink wine that night also, and the younger daughter went and lay with him.
Again he was not aware of it when she lay down or when she got up.

[36] So both of Lot's daughters became pregnant by their father. [37] The older daughter had a son, and she named him Moab; he is the father of the Moabites of today. [38] The younger daughter also had a son, and she named him Ben-Ammi; he is the father of the Ammonites of today.

ABRAHAM TESTED

[1] Some time later God tested Abraham. He said to him, "Abraham!"
"Here I am," he replied.
[2] Then God said, "Take your son, your only son, Isaac, whom you love, and go to the region of Moriah. Sacrifice him there as a burnt offering on one of the mountains I will tell you about."
[3] Early the next morning Abraham got up and saddled his donkey. He took with him two of his servants and his son Isaac. When he had cut enough wood for the burnt offering, he set out for the place God had told him about. [4] On the third day Abraham looked up and saw the place in the distance. [5] He said to his servants, "Stay here with the donkey while I and the boy go over there. We will worship and then we will come back to you."
[6] Abraham took the wood for the burnt offering and placed it on his son Isaac, and he himself carried the fire and the knife. As the two of them went on together, [7] Isaac spoke up and said to his father Abraham, "Father?"
"Yes, my son?" Abraham replied.
"The fire and wood are here," Isaac said, "but where is the lamb for the burnt offering?"
[8] Abraham answered, "God himself will provide the lamb for the burnt offering, my son." And the two of them went on together.

[9] When they reached the place God had told him about, Abraham built an altar there and arranged the wood on it. He bound his son Isaac and laid him on the altar, on top of the wood.

[10] Then he reached out his hand and took the knife to slay his son. [11] But the angel of the LORD called out to him from heaven, "Abraham! Abraham!"

"Here I am," he replied.

[12] "Do not lay a hand on the boy," he said. "Do not do anything to him. Now I know that you fear God, because you have not withheld from me your son, your only son."

[13] Abraham looked up and there in a thicket he saw a ram caught by its horns. He went over and took the ram and sacrificed it as a burnt offering instead of his son. [14] So Abraham called that place 'The LORD Will Provide.' And to this day it is said, 'On the mountain of the LORD it will be provided.'

[15] The angel of the LORD called to Abraham from heaven a second time [16] and said, "I swear by myself, declares the LORD, that because you have done this and have not withheld your son, your only son, [17] I will surely bless you and make your descendants as numerous as the stars in the sky and as the sand on the seashore. Your descendants will take possession of the cities of their enemies, [18] and through your offspring all nations on earth will be blessed, because you have obeyed me."

[19] Then Abraham returned to his servants, and they set off together for Beersheba. And Abraham stayed in Beersheba.

JACOB AND ESAU

[19] This is the account of Abraham's son Isaac. Abraham became the father of Isaac, [20] and Isaac was forty years old when he married Rebekah daughter of Bethuel the Aramean from Paddan Aram and sister of Laban the Aramean.

[21] Isaac prayed to the LORD on behalf of his wife, because she was barren. The LORD answered his prayer, and his wife Rebekah became pregnant. [22] The babies jostled each other within her, and she said, "Why is this happening to me?" So she went to inquire of the LORD.

[23] The LORD said to her, "Two nations are in your womb, and two peoples from within you will be separated; one people will be stronger than the other, and the older will serve the younger."

[24] When the time came for her to give birth, there were twin boys in her womb. [25] The first to come out was red, and his whole body was like a hairy garment; so they named him Esau. [26] After this, his brother came out, with his hand grasping Esau's heel; so he was named Jacob. Isaac was sixty years old when Rebekah gave birth to them.

[27] The boys grew up, and Esau became a skillful hunter, a man of the open country, while Jacob was a quiet man, staying among the tents.
[28] Isaac, who had a taste for wild game, loved Esau, but Rebekah loved Jacob.
[29] Once when Jacob was cooking some stew, Esau came in from the open country, famished. [30] He said to Jacob, "Quick, let me have some of that red stew! I'm famished!" That is why he was also called Edom.
[31] Jacob replied, "First sell me your birthright."
[32] "Look, I am about to die," Esau said. "What good is the birthright to me?"
[33] But Jacob said, "Swear to me first." So he swore an oath to him, selling his birthright to Jacob. [34] Then Jacob gave Esau some bread and some lentil stew. He ate and drank, and then got up and left.
So Esau despised his birthright.

JACOB GETS ISAAC'S BLESSING

[1] When Isaac was old and his eyes were so weak that he could no longer see, he called for Esau his older son and said to him, "My son."
"Here I am," he answered.
[2] Isaac said, "I am now an old man and don't know the day of my death. [3] Now then, get your weapons – your quiver and bow – and go out to the open country to hunt some wild game for me. [4] Prepare me the kind of tasty food I like and bring it to me to eat, so that I may give you my blessing before I die."
[5] Now Rebekah was listening as Isaac spoke to his son Esau. When Esau left for the open country to hunt game and bring it back, [6] Rebekah said to her son Jacob, "Look, I overheard your father say to your brother Esau, [7] 'Bring me some game and prepare me some tasty food to eat, so that I may give you my blessing in the presence of the LORD before I die.' [8] Now, my son, listen carefully and do what I tell you: [9] Go out to the flock and bring me two choice young goats, so I can prepare some tasty food for your father, just the way he likes it. [10] Then take it to your father to eat, so that he may give you his blessing before he dies."
[11] Jacob said to Rebekah his mother, "But my brother Esau is a hairy man, and I'm a man with smooth skin. [12] What if my father touches me? I would appear to be tricking him and would bring down a curse on myself rather than a blessing."
[13] His mother said to him, "My son, let the curse fall on me. Just do what I say; go and get them for me."
[14] So he went and got them and brought them to his mother, and she prepared some tasty food, just the way his father liked it. [15] Then Rebekah took the best clothes of Esau her older son, which she had in the house, and put them on her younger son Jacob. [16] She also covered his hands and the smooth part of his neck with the goatskins. [17] Then she handed to her son Jacob the tasty food and the bread she had made.
[18] He went to his father and said, "My father."
"Yes, my son," he answered. "Who is it?"
[19] Jacob said to his father, "I am Esau your firstborn. I have done as you told me. Please sit up and eat some of my game so that you may give me your blessing."
[20] Isaac asked his son, "How did you find it so quickly, my son?"
"The LORD your God gave me success," he replied.
[21] Then Isaac said to Jacob, "Come near so I can touch you, my son, to know whether you really are my son Esau or not."
[22] Jacob went close to his father Isaac, who touched him and said, "The voice is the voice of Jacob, but the hands are the hands of Esau." [23] He did not recognize him, for his hands were hairy like those of his brother Esau; so he blessed him. [24] "Are you really my son Esau?" he asked.
"I am," he replied.
[25] Then he said, "My son, bring me some of your game to eat, so that I may give you my blessing."
Jacob brought it to him and he ate; and he brought some wine and he drank. [26] Then his father Isaac said to him, "Come here, my son, and kiss me."
[27] So he went to him and kissed him. When Isaac caught the smell of his clothes, he blessed him and said, "Ah, the smell of my son is like the smell of a field that the LORD has blessed. [28] May God give you of heaven's dew and of earth's richness – an abundance of grain and new wine. [29] May nations serve you and peoples bow down to you. Be lord over your brothers, and may the sons of your mother bow down to you. May those who curse you be cursed and those who bless you be blessed."
[30] After Isaac finished blessing him and Jacob had scarcely left his father's presence, his brother Esau came in from hunting. [31] He too prepared some tasty food and brought it to his father. Then he said to him, "My father, sit up and eat some of my game, so that you may give me your blessing."
[32] His father Isaac asked him, "Who are you?"
"I am your son," he answered, "your firstborn, Esau."
[33] Isaac trembled violently and said, "Who was it, then, that hunted game and brought it to me? I ate it just before you came and I blessed him – and indeed he will be blessed!"
[34] When Esau heard his father's words, he burst out with a loud and bitter cry and said to his father, "Bless me – me too, my father!"
[35] But he said, "Your brother came deceitfully and took your blessing."
[36] Esau said, "Isn't he rightly named Jacob? He has deceived me these two times: He took my birthright, and now he's taken my blessing!" Then he asked, "Haven't you reserved any blessing for me?"
[37] Isaac answered Esau, "I have made him lord over you and have made all his relatives his servants, and I have sustained him with grain and new wine. So what can I possibly do for you, my son?"
[38] Esau said to his father, "Do you have only one blessing, my father? Bless me too, my father!" Then Esau wept aloud.
[39] His father Isaac answered him, "Your dwelling will be away from the earth's richness, away from the dew of heaven above. [40] You will live by the sword and you will serve your brother. But when you grow restless, you will throw his yoke from off your neck."

JACOB FLEES TO LABAN

[41] Esau held a grudge against Jacob because of the blessing his father had given him. He said to himself, "The days of mourning for my father are near; then I will kill my brother Jacob."
[42] When Rebekah was told what her older son Esau had said, she sent for her younger son Jacob and said to him, "Your brother Esau is consoling himself with the thought of killing you. [43] Now then, my son, do what I say: Flee at once to my brother Laban in Haran. [44] Stay with him for a while until your brother's fury subsides. [45] When your brother is no longer angry with you and forgets what you did to him, I'll send word for you to come back from there. Why should I lose both of you in one day?"
[46] Then Rebekah said to Isaac, "I'm disgusted with living because of these Hittite women. If Jacob takes a wife from among the women of this land, from Hittite women like these, my life will not be worth living."

RACHEL
LEAH
BILHAH
ZILPAH

JACOB'S CHILDREN

[31] When the LORD saw that Leah was not loved, he opened her womb, but Rachel was barren. [32] Leah became pregnant and gave birth to a son. She named him Reuben, for she said, "It is because the LORD has seen my misery. Surely my husband will love me now."
[33] She conceived again, and when she gave birth to a son she said, "Because the LORD heard that I am not loved, he gave me this one too." So she named him Simeon.
[34] Again she conceived, and when she gave birth to a son she said, "Now at last my husband will become attached to me, because I have borne him three sons." So he was named Levi.
[35] She conceived again, and when she gave birth to a son she said, "This time I will praise the LORD." So she named him Judah. Then she stopped having children.

[1] When Rachel saw that she was not bearing Jacob any children, she became jealous of her sister. So she said to Jacob, "Give me children, or I'll die!"
[2] Jacob became angry with her and said, "Am I in the place of God, who has kept you from having children?"
[3] Then she said, "Here is Bilhah, my maidservant. Sleep with her so that she can bear children for me and that through her I too can build a family."
[4] So she gave him her servant Bilhah as a wife. Jacob slept with her, [5] and she became pregnant and bore him a son. [6] Then Rachel said, "God has vindicated me; he has listened to my plea and given me a son." Because of this she named him Dan.
[7] Rachel's servant Bilhah conceived again and bore Jacob a second son. [8] Then Rachel said, "I have had a great struggle with my sister, and I have won." So she named him Naphtali.

[9] When Leah saw that she had stopped having children, she took her maidservant Zilpah and gave her to Jacob as a wife. [10] Leah's servant Zilpah bore Jacob a son. [11] Then Leah said, "What good fortune!" So she named him Gad.
[12] Leah's servant Zilpah bore Jacob a second son. [13] Then Leah said, "How happy I am! The women will call me happy." So she named him Asher.

[14] During wheat harvest, Reuben went out into the fields and found some mandrake plants, which he brought to his mother Leah. Rachel said to Leah, "Please give me some of your son's mandrakes."
[15] But she said to her, "Wasn't it enough that you took away my husband? Will you take my son's mandrakes too?"
"Very well," Rachel said, "he can sleep with you tonight in return for your son's mandrakes."

[16] So when Jacob came in from the fields that evening, Leah went out to meet him. "You must sleep with me," she said. "I have hired you with my son's mandrakes." So he slept with her that night.
[17] God listened to Leah, and she became pregnant and bore Jacob a fifth son. [18] Then Leah said, "God has rewarded me for giving my maidservant to my husband." So she named him Issachar.
[19] Leah conceived again and bore Jacob a sixth son. [20] Then Leah said, "God has presented me with a precious gift. This time my husband will treat me with honor, because I have borne him six sons." So she named him Zebulun.
[21] Some time later she gave birth to a daughter and named her Dinah.
[22] Then God remembered Rachel; he listened to her and opened her womb. [23] She became pregnant and gave birth to a son and said, "God has taken away my disgrace." [24] She named him Joseph, and said, "May the LORD add to me another son."

RACHEL
LEAH
BILHAH
ZILPAH
1
2
4
5
6
7
8
9
10
11

JACOB WRESTLES WITH GOD

22 That night Jacob got up and took his two wives, his two maidservants and his eleven sons and crossed the ford of the Jabbok. 23 After he had sent them across the stream, he sent over all his possessions.
24 So Jacob was left alone, and a man wrestled with him till daybreak. 25 When the man saw that he could not overpower him, he touched the socket of Jacob's hip so that his hip was wrenched as he wrestled with the man. 26 Then the man said, "Let me go, for it is daybreak."
But Jacob replied, "I will not let you go unless you bless me."
27 The man asked him, "What is your name?"
"Jacob," he answered.
28 Then the man said, "Your name will no longer be Jacob, but Israel, because you have struggled with God and with men and have overcome."
29 Jacob said, "Please tell me your name."
But he replied, "Why do you ask my name?" Then he blessed him there.
30 So Jacob called the place Peniel, saying, "It is because I saw God face to face, and yet my life was spared."
31 The sun rose above him as he passed Peniel, and he was limping because of his hip. 32 Therefore to this day the Israelites do not eat the tendon attached to the socket of the hip, because the socket of Jacob's hip was touched near the tendon.

OUCH!

JACOB MEETS ESAU

[1] Jacob looked up and there was Esau, coming with his four hundred men; so he divided the children among Leah, Rachel and the two maidservants. [2] He put the maidservants and their children in front, Leah and her children next, and Rachel and Joseph in the rear. [3] He himself went on ahead and bowed down to the ground seven times as he approached his brother.

[4] But Esau ran to meet Jacob and embraced him; he threw his arms around his neck and kissed him. And they wept. [5] Then Esau looked up and saw the women and children. "Who are these with you?" he asked. Jacob answered, "They are the children God has graciously given your servant."

[6] Then the maidservants and their children approached and bowed down.

[7] Next, Leah and her children came and bowed down. Last of all came Joseph and Rachel, and they too bowed down.

[8] Esau asked, "What do you mean by all these droves I met?"

"To find favor in your eyes, my lord," he said.

[9] But Esau said, "I already have plenty, my brother. Keep what you have for yourself."

[10] "No, please!" said Jacob. "If I have found favor in your eyes, accept this gift from me. For to see your face is like seeing the face of God, now that you have received me favorably. [11] Please accept the present that was brought to you, for God has been gracious to me and I have all I need." And because Jacob insisted, Esau accepted it.

[12] Then Esau said, "Let us be on our way; I'll accompany you."

[13] But Jacob said to him, "My lord knows that the children are tender and that I must care for the ewes and cows that are nursing their young. If they are driven hard just one day, all the animals will die. [14] So let my lord go on ahead of his servant, while I move along slowly at the pace of the droves before me and that of the children, until I come to my lord in Seir."

[15] Esau said, "Then let me leave some of my men with you."

"But why do that?" Jacob asked. "Just let me find favor in the eyes of my lord."

[16] So that day Esau started on his way back to Seir. [17] Jacob, however, went to Succoth, where he built a place for himself and made shelters for his livestock. That is why the place is called Succoth.

[18] After Jacob came from Paddan Aram, he arrived safely at the city of Shechem in Canaan and camped within sight of the city. [19] For a hundred pieces of silver, he bought from the sons of Hamor, the father of Shechem, the plot of ground where he pitched his tent. [20] There he set up an altar and called it El Elohe Israel.

JACOB BLESSES HIS SONS

[1] Then Jacob called for his sons and said: "Gather around so I can tell you what will happen to you in days to come. [2] Assemble and listen, sons of Jacob; listen to your father Israel.
[3] Reuben, you are my firstborn, my might, the first sign of my strength, excelling in honor, excelling in power. [4] Turbulent as the waters, you will no longer excel, for you went up onto your father's bed, onto my couch and defiled it.
[5] Simeon and Levi are brothers – their swords are weapons of violence. [6] Let me not enter their council, let me not join their assembly, for they have killed men in their anger and hamstrung oxen as they pleased. [7] Cursed be their anger, so fierce, and their fury, so cruel! I will scatter them in Jacob and disperse them in Israel.
[8] Judah, your brothers will praise you; your hand will be on the neck of your enemies; your father's sons will bow down to you. [9] You are a lion's cub, O Judah; you return from the prey, my son. Like a lion he crouches and lies down, like a lioness – who dares to rouse him? [10] The scepter will not depart from Judah, nor the ruler's staff from between his feet, until he comes to whom it belongs and the obedience of the nations is his. [11] He will tether his donkey to a vine, his colt to the choicest branch; he will wash his garments in wine, his robes in the blood of grapes. [12] His eyes will be darker than wine, his teeth whiter than milk.
[13] Zebulun will live by the seashore and become a haven for ships; his border will extend toward Sidon.
[14] Issachar is a rawboned donkey lying down between two saddlebags. [15] When he sees how good is his resting place and how pleasant is his land, he will bend his shoulder to the burden and submit to forced labor.
[16] Dan will provide justice for his people as one of the tribes of Israel. [17] Dan will be a serpent by the roadside, a viper along the path, that bites the horse's heels so that its rider tumbles backward. [18] I look for your deliverance, O LORD.
[19] Gad will be attacked by a band of raiders, but he will attack them at their heels.
[20] Asher's food will be rich; he will provide delicacies fit for a king.
[21] Naphtali is a doe set free that bears beautiful fawns.
[22] Joseph is a fruitful vine, a fruitful vine near a spring, whose branches climb over a wall. [23] With bitterness archers attacked him; they shot at him with hostility. [24] But his bow remained steady, his strong arms stayed limber, because of the hand of the Mighty One of Jacob, because of the Shepherd, the Rock of Israel, [25] because of your father's God, who helps you, because of the Almighty, who blesses you with blessings of the heavens above, blessings of the deep that lies below, blessings of the breast and womb. [26] Your father's blessings are greater than the blessings of the ancient mountains, than the bounty of the age-old hills. Let all these rest on the head of Joseph, on the brow of the prince among his brothers.
[27] Benjamin is a ravenous wolf; in the morning he devours the prey, in the evening he divides the plunder."
[28] All these are the twelve tribes of Israel, and this is what their father said to them when he blessed them, giving each the blessing appropriate to him.

12
11
10
9
8
7
1
2
3
4
5
6

THE DEATH OF JACOB

[29] Then he gave them these instructions: "I am about to be gathered to my people. Bury me with my fathers in the cave in the field of Ephron the Hittite, [30] the cave in the field of Machpelah, near Mamre in Canaan, which Abraham bought as a burial place from Ephron the Hittite, along with the field. [31] There Abraham and his wife Sarah were buried, there Isaac and his wife Rebekah were buried, and there I buried Leah. [32] The field and the cave in it were bought from the Hittites."
[33] When Jacob had finished giving instructions to his sons, he drew his feet up into the bed, breathed his last and was gathered to his parents.

[1] Joseph threw himself upon his father and wept over him and kissed him. [2] Then Joseph directed the physicians in his service to embalm his father Israel. So the physicians embalmed him, [3] taking a full forty days, for that was the time required for embalming. And the Egyptians mourned for him seventy days.
[4] When the days of mourning had passed, Joseph said to Pharaoh's court, "If I have found favor in your eyes, speak to Pharaoh for me. Tell him, [5] 'My father made me swear an oath and said, "I am about to die; bury me in the tomb I dug for myself in the land of Canaan." Now let me go up and bury my father; then I will return.' "
[6] Pharaoh said, "Go up and bury your father, as he made you swear to do."
[7] So Joseph went up to bury his father. All Pharaoh's officials accompanied him – the dignitaries of his court and all the dignitaries of Egypt – [8] besides all the members of Joseph's household and his brothers and those belonging to his father's household. Only their children and their flocks and herds were left in Goshen. [9] Chariots and horsemen also went up with him. It was a very large company.
[10] When they reached the threshing floor of Atad, near the Jordan, they lamented loudly and bitterly; and there Joseph observed a seven-day period of mourning for his father. [11] When the Canaanites who lived there saw the mourning at the threshing floor of Atad, they said, "The Egyptians are holding a solemn ceremony of mourning." That is why that place near the Jordan is called Abel Mizraim.
[12] So Jacob's sons did as he had commanded them: [13] They carried him to the land of Canaan and buried him in the cave in the field of Machpelah, near Mamre, which Abraham had bought as a burial place from Ephron the Hittite, along with the field. [14] After burying his father, Joseph returned to Egypt, together with his brothers and all the others who had gone with him to bury his father.

THE CREATION
Pictures from the Book of Genesis

by CHRISTIAN MONTENEGRO
www.christianmontenegro.com.ar

Edited by Robert Klanten, Hendrik Hellige, Birga Meyer

Project Management by Hendrik Hellige
Production Management by Janni Milstrey
Layout by Birga Meyer

Published by Die Gestalten Verlag, Berlin · London, 2004
ISBN 3-89955-034-X

Printed by Medialis, Berlin. Made in Germany.

For more information please check: www.die-gestalten.de